Unlearning Failure

Unlearning Failure

Can Urban Schools Be Transformed in the New Millennium?

Dierdre G. Paul

ROWMAN & LITTLEFIELD
Lanham • Boulder • New York • London

Published by Rowman & Littlefield
An imprint of The Rowman & Littlefield Publishing Group, Inc.
4501 Forbes Boulevard, Suite 200, Lanham, Maryland 20706
https://rowman.com

6 Tinworth Street, London SE11 5AL, United Kingdom

Copyright © 2019 by Dierdre G. Paul

All rights reserved. No part of this book may be reproduced in any form or by any electronic or mechanical means, including information storage and retrieval systems, without written permission from the publisher, except by a reviewer who may quote passages in a review.

British Library Cataloguing in Publication Information Available

Library of Congress Cataloging-in-Publication Data

Includes bibliographic references
ISBN 978-1-4758-3556-4 (cloth : alk. paper)
ISBN 978-1-4758-3557-1 (pbk. : alk. paper)
ISBN 978-1-4758-3558-8 (electronic)

∞ ™ The paper used in this publication meets the minimum requirements of American National Standard for Information Sciences Permanence of Paper for Printed Library Materials, ANSI/NISO Z39.48-1992.

This book is dedicated to my grandmother, Mrs. Mary Helen Pinkard,
April 5, 1902–February 16, 2018

Contents

Preface	ix
Acknowledgments	xvii
Introduction	xix

Part I: Unlearning Failure?   1

1. Demythologizing the American History of Urban Public Schooling   3
2. The Emergence of Race in the Debate on Urban School Reform   17
3. The Infusion of Big, Federal Cash . . . Throwing Good Money after Bad   29

Part II: Can Urban Schools Be Transformed in the New Millennium?   43

4. Can Failure Be Unlearned?: Can Urban Schools Actually Be Transformed in the New Millennium?   45
5. Can Competition Serve as the Jump Start That Failing Urban Public Schools Need to Get Their Acts Together?   61
6. What Is School Choice?: Why Is It the Only Viable Alternative to Failing Urban Schools in the New Millennium?   77

References	95
About the Author	101

Preface

> The book represents my point of view at a particular moment. It stands still; I hope my thinking doesn't. (Katz, 1971, 1975, xiii)

The subject of urban educational renewal has intrigued me for some time now. After all, I attended urban public schools in the Bronx, New York, until tenth grade, when I received a full ride to Miss Hall's School in Pittsfield, Massachusetts, through the *A Better Chance* program (*ABC*). In many respects, *ABC* could be considered a voucher program of sorts.

Started in 1963, *ABC* offers many students of color the "chance" to leave oftentimes failing local public schools to attend high-quality private and public schools throughout the United States. *ABC* has grown exponentially over time. At its inception in 1963, the fledgling program enrolled a mere fifty-five students in nine schools. During AY 2015–2016, however, the program boasted of having placed more than two thousand students at approximately 350 top-notch private and public schools nationally (Grossberg, 2017).

Upon finishing college and with the belief that joining the ranks of public school teachers would be temporary, I returned to the same Bronx community in which I grew up . . . to teach this time. I taught in a Bronx intermediate school for six and a half years. Then I was promoted to communication arts teacher trainer in a Bronx elementary school near Yankee Stadium during my seventh year in the profession. I remained there for one year until I became a teacher educator at Montclair State University (MSU) in Upper Montclair, New Jersey.

I have been at MSU ever since, and although there have been a couple of turbulent times (as expected in any work setting), I have always considered my work at the university to be my life's mission and the opportunity to work there (for the most part happily) to be a blessing. During my twenty-five years at Montclair State, I have encountered thousands of teachers who teach in every one of New Jersey's twenty-one counties and many of its 590 school districts, including urban centers like Paterson, Jersey City, Elizabeth, Trenton, Perth Amboy, and Newark.

I have also conducted on-site professional development for teachers and principals in both Newark and Paterson. I was selected to participate in action research spearheaded by John Goodlad's National Network for Educational Renewal in Seattle, Washington, in addition to serving as a member of numerous educationally driven organizations with the expressed mission of improving urban schools.

So it is an understatement to say that I have had a lot of experience working with urban school districts. For an even longer period of time, however, I have had the opportunity to analyze and study the problems inherent to educating students in urban school districts. Yet all of this involvement and work toward improving the quality of urban schools has led to a very sad realization.

No sugarcoating here. These schools are just as bad today (if not worse) than they were twenty-five years ago when I left public school teaching. Absent hyperbole, the state of urban public schools throughout the United States is a huge, almost impenetrable mess that is also polemical and politically divisive.

There are those who contend that, despite flagging standardized test scores and through-the-roof dropout rates, urban center schools are doing better than expected. Ironically, while citing quixotic praise for the urban schools where they frequently work and/or provide services, many of the same school champions have not sent and will not send their own children to the schools that they deem "good enough" for other people's children.

For example, it is nothing short of bizarre that, despite the full-throated defense of public schools and a reaffirmation of progress that few others have seen, Presidents Obama and Clinton and Senators Kennedy and Durbin all sent their children to private schools. It seems to me that this glaring contradiction pays homage to the Orwell quote, "All animals are equal, but some animals are more equal than others."

Further, these advocates make the claim that real and sustained change is not possible until the attendant social ills (that is, poverty, crime, childhood hunger) plaguing many of these communities are competently addressed. Since the inception of the United States, however, when have these social ills ever been totally eradicated? Even better, please name a single industrialized nation that has completely eliminated them.

The floating of this utopian dream is what prompts many to totally dismiss the solutions to urban school reform that liberals and those referring to themselves as the Left present with a serious face. First, these putative solutions lack pragmatism and details that are specific to their effective implementation. Second, and a far greater problem, is the liberal tendency to spend other people's money (taxpayer dollars) in the advancement of what they alone cast as moral and socially just.

Conversely, critics of urban public schools cite the lack of results (using standard and widely accepted metrics) as conclusive proof that—despite our best efforts—we are not succeeding with these schools or these youngsters. Essentially, we are throwing good money after bad, and the problems plaguing these school districts remain intransigent regardless of the amount of money thrown at them.

Historically, this argument between the two sides has devolved rapidly. Yet the devolution accelerated even quicker when the polarized sides started to cast the issue in moral terms. More frequently, liberals tended to characterize those concerned about the cost-ineffectiveness of urban education and critical of its lack of tangible results as being *morally wrong, culturally insensitive, racist,* and/or *tightfisted*. Without exception, such characterizations are pejorative, presumptuous, and do relatively little to move the needle.

I reject the premise that one can make any judgment about another's morality on the basis of a single issue. Therefore, we should choose instead to see those perceptions that differ from our own as "different" rather than "deficient." Oftentimes, heated, hypercritical arguments (like this one) unintentionally widen the chasm between people whose interests might otherwise be aligned. Saddest of all, these arguments fail to yield realistic solutions that help us to substantively think about workable solutions or effectuate real and sustained change.

So the bottom line is: This issue regarding urban schooling is not a new one for me. Yet it is also fair to state that, as life "happened," the issue moved from the foreground to the background. Yet its importance was recently thrust back into my consciousness with help from a rather unlikely source, New Jersey governor Christopher J. Christie.

Although many anticipated that the governor would go quietly into the night (post–presidential bid), those of us in the Garden State knew differently. After closely observing him for eight years, we knew that those suggesting that he would shrink from the public glare and take a backseat were just flat out wrong.

The situation in particular that grabbed my attention started on June 21, 2016, when Governor Chris Christie kicked off his School Funding Fairness Tour, composed of a series of town hall meetings held throughout the state. The tour afforded the governor the chance to take his case directly to the people regarding school funding problems in New Jersey.

Quite simply expressed, here were the highpoints of his case: *The state's school funding formula—based on the School Funding Reform Act (SFRA) of*

2008—is irreparably broken. It is in desperate need of a more equitable distribution of school aid for each student. Governor Christie therefore proposed a flat rate in the amount of $6,599 for every K–12 student, while maintaining funding levels for students with special needs.

As anticipated, Governor Christie's new plan garnered a good deal of attention from the local press, in addition to the expected scorn and praise from the public. The political fault lines were firmly drawn. The state's teachers' unions and Democratic legislators (representing New Jersey's largest urban school districts) predictably slammed the plan as "heartless" and intentionally hurting urban students. Conversely, Republican legislators and the clear majority of New Jersey taxpayers were cautiously optimistic about the prospect of seeing their property tax bills lowered.

Most New Jersey taxpayers will take property tax relief any way we can get it. Again in 2017, New Jersey earned the distinction of being ranked first in the nation for having the highest property taxes. That distinction has seemingly remained static over the years, despite the enactment of a 2010 bipartisan law lowering the rate of property tax increases from 4 percent to 2 percent annually. Additionally, the state's elevated property taxes are directly correlated with the widely disparate school funding most of the state's municipalities and townships receive. Education is the single greatest cost driver for local municipalities.

Several months later, during his February 28, 2017, *Final Budget Address*, Governor Christie reiterated his central premise on this issue that "school funding in New Jersey is not fair." In past iterations, the governor had accurately described the current school funding formula as "more confusing than the formula for old Coke." The most important feature of the governor's final budget address, however, was his direct challenge to the New Jersey State Legislature and the establishment of a timeline for action.

While critics of Governor Christie's original school funding proposal have been quick to attribute malintent to those amenable to making the existing formula more equitable, few (including the Democrat-controlled New Jersey State Legislature) appear oblivious to the fact that New Jersey's current school funding formula simply does not work. The budget numbers cannot sustain full funding. In fact, the SFRA of 2008 has not been fully funded since its inception.

To their credit, the New Jersey Senate and Assembly leaders heeded the governor's caution and accepted his challenge. Both houses of the legislature put forth their own distinctive school funding plans that their members—and the constituencies they represent—considered far less draconian than the one proffered by Christie.

In the end, however, the final bill that was passed—after a three-day government shutdown—did little to address the issues of school funding in New Jersey. Key aspects of the bill included funding of the SFRA for the first time since its inception in 2008, as well as $150 million in new school aid (specifically $100 million for K–12 schools, $25 million for preschool expansion, and $25 million for special education).

At first glance, some might characterize this outcome as a victory, especially those who are laser focused on the fact that the SFRA would be fully funded for the first time under Governor Christie. Yet many people remain incredibly disheartened due the shortsightedness of the solution, as well as the fact that it is fiscally unsustainable. Further, it additionally taxes an already overtaxed populace and works from the faulty premise that the proverbial "free lunch" actually exists when, in actuality, free lunches are always paid for by someone else.

Although there was a real chance to address the issue of school funding in New Jersey during 2017, that opportunity vanished when legislators lost sight of the goal and instead chose to focus on political theatrics and jockeying for position in 2018 rather than on what is best for the state's school children and their families.

So now we are stuck a while longer with a mortally flawed school funding plan that does little to address the quality of education students receive, especially in the state's urban centers where a high-quality education should be privileged most. Pragmatically, the slightly revamped plan will do little more than perpetuate the educationally harmful practices employed by those New Jersey school districts with historically bad fiscal stewardship and poor educational outcomes.

It is this situation in New Jersey that reminded me of how rarely true reform occurs in urban public school systems, despite infusing them with grossly disproportionate amounts of state school aid. While each election cycle brings about a new promise to revamp public education, that promise quickly transfigures into little more than a dream deferred.

During this latest of New Jersey's budget crises, one fact clearly emerged. There seems to be no true will or resolve among most of New Jersey's politicians to actually do the work involved in making *all* schools work for the state's students, especially those in urban centers who have long been victims of the substandard schooling they receive.

Of course, the school funding problems and urban education dilemmas in New Jersey are not distinctive and I am not making the claim that they are. Rather, they are illustrative of the school-based difficulties experienced by myriad other urban public school systems throughout the United States.

Yet here's what the situation in New Jersey distinctively did for me. It sparked an inquisitiveness and made me wonder about the origins of the problems we presently face with our urban public schools. I pondered whether the dilemma's attributes had evolved over time or essentially remained the same since the inception of US public schools. I was curious about the point at which the issue of race first surfaced in the debate and took on the primacy that it presently holds.

That curiosity then led me to research and complete a historical analysis on urban school reform throughout the United States. In the process, I learned that urban schools have always been problematic. Specifically, the problems associated with educating children and youth growing up in America's inner cities can be traced to the early 1800s. During the nineteenth and early twentieth centuries, however, the difficulties were seemingly situated in students' socioeconomic status.

While those youngsters were poor in most instances, they were not predominantly black and Hispanic as they are today. Therefore, the nexus of race and socioeconomic status may have played a far greater role in the substandard quality of education those students received than either factor played individually. Race doesn't emerge as a factor until post-1954, after the *Brown* cases had been ruled upon.

Over the course of time, we have floated many remedies to what ails the urban public schools to no avail. In the end, not much has worked or been sustained . . . and for this author, there simply is no more time to waste. How many more urban center generations must be lost because of the inferior schools to which they have been relegated?

To me, to have generational cycles of failure perpetuated is the most virulent expression of racism. So this book provides a vehicle for me to float other options that are based on a free market principle. If the public schools in these urban centers continue to provide low-quality and subpar educational opportunities for their students and the problem has generationally existed without abatement, they need to shut down.

My belief is, despite pleas from teachers' unions and others satisfied with the status quo in these failing schools to provide them with time to fix the schools, we've waited for far too long. So at this point all options should be on the table, including vouchers, educational savings accounts, and charter schools. These suffering families and students deserve to feel hopeful again and be well educated enough to actually break the cycle of poverty with which they've put up for far too long.

So *Unlearning Failure* provides rather unconventional solutions to this problem of urban school failure. Some might even consider them draconian . . . and so what if they are? The time for change is now and we have no more time to wait. "The revolution will not be televised" (Scott-Heron, 1970).

I also have an admission to make about writing this book. It more than any other I have written thus far made me afraid. Why? There are a host of reasons, but chief among them is the fact that many of the books and articles I wrote earlier in my academic career were very simple to write. I simply parroted back the Leftist ideologies I learned as a young scholar at the liberal graduate schools I attended and from more well-established scholars who shared my affinity for those philosophies.

I was accustomed to friends and mentors telling me to tone down the rhetoric for fear that I would be cast as an ideologue. That didn't bother me, however, because I was a true believer and I had a unidimensional view of the world and life that usually accompanies youth. I unquestioningly accepted the rhetoric of the Democratic Party and its affiliates (that is, labor unions).

Then life got in the way of the fantasy. Over time and with a lot of quite valuable life experience, I came to several compelling realizations. Number one is that it's easy to demand income equality when you have no real money of your own and you're dictating the terms of what other people should do with their money that they have frequently worked hard for.

Two is that there is no free money. In order to raise two children to adulthood as a single, divorced mother, I was obligated to live within my means and pay as I went. So the value of money and fiscal sanity began to take hold of my life. I also came to a related realization as a property taxpayer. I was simply seeing too little return on investment for the taxes I paid and started to slowly become angry at what I viewed as the waste and mismanagement of money I sent to both my state and federal governments.

Add to those facts that I have and maintain a deep and abiding respect and admiration for my faith as a Catholic, it deeply saddened me to see New Jersey Catholic schools that had so well served both of my children throughout their K–12 education struggling for financial existence and to keep their doors open.

I wrote *Unlearning Failure* because I am now willing to take the risk of saying what desperately needs to be said about the failing state of urban public schooling that appears to have been and remains on a downward trajectory, despite momentous legal battles and massive infusions of federal funding. At the end of the day, the efforts to right the ship (albeit heroic) have failed, and these children and families simply have no more time to waste while others "get it right."

So I write, and that writing is motivated by my deep and abiding commitment to children and my desire for all of them to receive high-quality educational experiences, regardless of ZIP code or socioeconomic status. To echo the words of Condoleezza Rice, the issue of quality education is the civil rights issue of our time.

Acknowledgments

I will start by thanking Tom Koerner for believing in this book and me, and also for his patience and kindness. Thank you to Carlie Wall as well.

I would like to thank my graduate assistant Jacqueline Araneo for her editorial skills and for helping me ensure that the numbers were crisp for the preface and chapters 1 through 3.

I would like to thank my mother, my sister, and my children for their unending love and support.

I often refrain from acknowledging personal relationships as a matter of principle. The reason is specific to the fact that some enter our lives for a reason with a particular set of lessons to teach and others remain for the long haul. Yet, I feel compelled to acknowledge you, J. T. During our time together, you have taught me so much about love, sincerity, and you make me feel truly needed. I hope we stand the test of time, together.

Introduction

Unlearning Failure: Can Urban Schools Be Transformed in the New Millennium? follows a pattern emergent in the author's work and it is reflective of a mind-set she has established over time. She wholeheartedly believes that while it is critically important to define and clearly understand all of the dynamics inherent to society's most intransigent problems, it is just as critically important to proffer viable solutions.

For example, there is little disagreement witnessed when educators, politicians, or the general public (for that matter) are confronted with the statement that the dearth of equitable educational opportunities for far too many black and Hispanic youngsters in urban centers now constitutes a national crisis.

In fact, as outlined in the preface, some have even cast this societal failure as the most pressing civil rights issue of our time and one necessitating the serious consideration of all viable options. So *Unlearning Failure* will devote more time and writing space to possibility thinking and devising workable answers than it will to regurgitating well-known claims and recalibrating existing problems.

By wasting time with excessive definition and redefinition of stubbornly persistent problems, we simply perpetuate cycles of educational failure with which too many communities of color have lived for far too long. This book seeks to leave the reader feeling optimistic and forward thinking about our collective ability to provide a better educational future for all of our children.

Rather than simply reciting problems, *Unlearning Failure* seeks to explore credible solutions. If we are to fix the current urban schooling mess that we find ourselves in, we might well need to reignite our collective outside-the-box thinking as well as revisit measures previously labeled controversial.

The answers proposed aren't intended to serve as panaceas, nor does the author believe that the reader will (necessarily) agree with all of the options proffered, especially as she isn't seeking lockstep agreement. For instance, some of the answers include an exploration of charter schools and school choice voucher programs. While such solutions are hotly contested, they shouldn't be outright dismissed until all of the facts surrounding them have been disseminated, as opposed to those selectively put forth by those with a vested interest in propping up these "factories of failure," as Rist (1973) referred to them and which remains relevant today.

Therefore, part I of the book seeks to contextualize and analyze the vast array of problems (historical as well as contemporary) that have plagued urban schools. The other half is devoted to finding answers.

The central premise of chapter 1, "Demythologizing the American History of Urban Public Schooling," is outlined as follows. While we should acknowledge the sizable role that race has played and continues to play in the history of urban school reform, the dilemma's class-based dimensions shouldn't be overlooked, nor should the fact that race often assumes a synergistic and intersectional impact when paired with socioeconomic status.

Chapter 2, "The Emergence of Race in the Debate on Urban School Reform," challenges the extent of the role that race actually played then and continues to play presently. When making the rather flimsy case for maintaining failing urban public schools and continuing to disserve urban families and communities of color, the argument put forth by some is predicated on the big bad wolf of racism. There is a near hyperbolic contention that racial animus has been the sole driver with respect to funding and other disparities between urban, suburban, and rural school districts throughout the nation.

Chapter 2 submits that race might not yet have taken on such historical primacy in past explorations of urban school reform conducted during the late nineteenth and much of the twentieth centuries. The dilemma of inferior schooling in urban centers has been intractably persistent and commenced prior to the point that large numbers of students of color actually started attending them.

Chapter 3, "The Infusion of Big, Federal Cash . . . Throwing Good Money after Bad," picks up where the preceding chapter left off, with the introduction of the Civil Rights Act of 1964 (CRA). The context in which the CRA was explored in chapter 2 centered on its use as a compliance tool (in the form of monetary penalty) to force those schools continuing to resist enforcement of *Brown* to acquiesce.

Further, while chapter 3 rather briefly discusses CRA, it more deeply scrutinizes the strength of subsequent and costlier federal interventions that directly impacted public education, generally, and seem to have exacerbated the urban public school crisis, in particular.

Part II (chapters 4 through 6) is devoted to building the argument for a paradigm shift, as well as the proffering of educational alternatives and new, viable options that will undoubtedly turn failing public schools around.

Chapter 4, "Can Failure Be Unlearned?: Can Urban Schools Actually Be Transformed in the New Millennium?," poses two central questions that drive its scholarly exploration. One of this chapter's major premises centers on the fact that those who support consistently failing schools are incapable of unlearning failure for it is, quite simply, too ingrained and now functions as a new normal for them. Conversely, those most vulnerable and highly susceptible, the students attending and their families, have been most harmed by the longitudinal effects of this toxic schooling.

Although it obviously isn't working for the students trapped within them and left with relatively few educational alternatives, the pervasive and long-standing failure of urban schools is apparently working quite well for some, like American teacher unions. It also demonstrates the present state of disrepair in which urban schools find themselves, as evidenced by a snapshot of the educational outcomes of some of the nation's largest contemporary urban public school districts.

The chapter concludes with the following prognosis. There are some urban public schools for which there are no quick fixes or easy solutions. Those schools are simply too far gone, and radical alternatives must be explored if the students who have been generationally trapped in these schools are to have a fighting chance.

Chapter 5, "Can Competition Serve as the Jump Start That Failing Urban Public Schools Need to Get Their Acts Together?," seeks to establish the necessity of market-driven competition as a means of enhancing the overall quality of urban public schools. Further, the chapter makes the hard-charging point that high-quality schools should be capable of withstanding both competition and accountability. In those instances where they can't match up, however, their doors should close and they should cease to exist.

Yet the reader should also be clear that this book in no way espouses or advocates for the destruction of public education as we know it, although that desire to see urban public schools that can demonstrate their efficacy remain in the business of educating youngsters doesn't negate the following fact. Too many urban public schools continue to fail. It also doesn't change the fact that not all of the community's public schools are needed, especially in those instances in which they aren't properly functioning and have failed to do so for quite some time now.

So this chapter advances the thought that students in urban centers should no longer be hamstringed by their ZIP codes. It argues that those students be presented with the same educational options and choices that more affluent parents (in higher tax brackets) have afforded their children for quite some time now because they have the resources to do so. Just because many urban parents/caregivers don't have that same access to cash doesn't mean that their children should be forced to tolerate inferior schooling that has failed them for generations at this point in time.

Chapter 6, "What Is School Choice?: Why Is It the Only Viable Alternative to Failing Urban Schools in the New Millennium?," is focused on defining traditional iterations of school choice, in addition to presenting a contemporary and enhanced array of educational options that include charter schools, homeschooling, tuition tax credits and deductions, and vouchers.

Part I

Unlearning Failure?

Chapter One

Demythologizing the American History of Urban Public Schooling

> Myths die hard in America. Most tenacious are those that pertain to notions about our national character, our role in international affairs, and the society we envision ourselves as having built. Common to all of them is the aggrandizement of a supposed virtue that sets us apart as distinct and unique people.... As a consequence of what we believe ourselves to be, we have effectively blocked or ignored that which might demythologize what we know to be "real." (Rist, 1973, p. 1)

When the topic of present-day failing urban schools is raised, it's usually cast as a new phenomenon and one that is seemingly devoid of historical context. Additionally, many of those broaching the topic would have us believe that urban school failure and disrepair are solely predicated upon the race of the students attending them. They assert that the poor quality of schooling received in modern-day urban centers is specially linked to racial discrimination against students who are predominantly Hispanic and black.

Yes, that argument holds kernels of truth. Without a doubt, there is a racial *component* inherent. Although it has become transmutable over time, race has always played a demonstrably palpable role in the fabric of America and it always will. *Race* still matters (Paul, 2017). Today, it has simply "become metaphorical—a way of referring to and disguising forces, events, classes and expressions of social decay and economic division far more threatening to the body politic than biological 'race' ever was" (Morrison, 1992, p. 63).

But to make racism the central issue in any debate regarding the failure of contemporary urban school systems is to disregard the fact that people of color have made many strides and we now live in an America that stands in stark contrast to the America of the past, an America plagued by racial injustice and horrific acts solely motivated by racial animus and widespread societal discord (Paul, 2017).

Additionally, our young people aren't growing up in "that" America of the past. They are growing up and attending school in a pluralistic society. "Our nation is more racially/ethnically diverse than it has ever been, as are our schools. And while managing the heterogeneity of our broader society and the schools is knotty and multifaceted, it is also refreshing, rewarding and reflective of growth" (Paul, 2017, p. 2). So equating today's racial discrimination with that of our racially torturous past sets up a false equivalency.

Therefore, we should acknowledge the sizable role that race has played and continues to play in the history of American schooling; however, we shouldn't overlook the dilemma's class-based dimensions or the fact that race often assumes a synergistic and intersectional impact when paired with socioeconomic status.

There is another relevant distinction made in this discussion as well, and it centers on the difference between education and schooling. This book focuses on schooling, as "not all schooling is education nor education, schooling. The proper subject of concern is education. The activities of the government are mostly limited to schooling" (Friedman, 1962, p. 86).

RACE AND EDUCATION IN COLONIAL AMERICA

The race of black and Native American learners played a pivotal role in the way both groups were educated in colonial America. In 1619, most blacks who immigrated to the thirteen colonies did so as indentured servants rather than as slaves (Webb, 2006). By 1775—the start of the Revolutionary War—however, a seismic shift occurred, and the new majority of blacks were slaves.

Prior to the reversal, missionary groups provided the bulk of schooling experiences received by both blacks and Native Americans (Webb, 2006). And while this effort should be noted for historical accuracy, it was statistically irrelevant as it didn't result in large numbers of either group being formally educated. Some estimates suggest that 5 percent of slaves were literate in 1860 just prior to the Civil War, although there is no way to verify that statistic (Webb, 2006).

For all intents and purposes, the deleterious impact of slavery on educational opportunities for blacks was far more consequential. Upon arrival to the unfamiliar colonial shores of the United States, the enslaved had their lack of facility with a new oral language exploited for the purpose of maintaining social control and bolstering societal stratification. It was a common practice for enslavers to mix different tribes of Africans within slave communities to minimize the possibility of insurrection; it was also a form of psychological terrorism used to manipulate and create disequilibrium (Paul, 2016).

Despite the massive obstacles encountered, however, the enslaved quickly learned to use oral language in ways that bridged aspects of their native tongues with Standard American and British English. Then the goal post was figuratively moved and the focal point shifted to denying the enslaved literacy. Slaves' acquisition of literacy, the ability and willingness to use reading and writing to construct meaning, posed an even greater threat to the extant social order. Thus, that heightened threat resulted in literacy teaching of or by the enslaved being designated a capital offense (by law) in many regions of the pre–Civil War South (Paul, 2016).

Some contended that the impetus for literacy's prohibition was a spike in the number of slave insurrections and the concomitant proliferation of abolitionist pamphlets and tracts that were feared for their potential power to agitate the enslaved (Paul, 2000). While it is highly probable that the insurrections and tracts did cause slaveholders alarm, it is indisputable that social control and the perpetuation of a system dependent upon the economic exploitation of black people also served as weighty considerations in enacting and perpetuating the prohibition.

Yet there is an important diversionary note to be made at this point in the discussion. Within the context of this examination, there is no effort to solely cast the enslaved as "victims" of the slave trade. Although one must acknowledge that enslaved Africans were victimized and terrorized, it is also true that they resisted and devised *emancipatory literacies*, which demonstrated their resistance (Paul, 2016). Thus, while recounting the horrors and process of dehumanization they suffered, it becomes equally important to deconstruct victimhood narratives.

In viewing literacy as a technology (Gee and Hayes, 2011) or the mode of transmission through which oral language and thought are conveyed, one is able to identify various ways through which the enslaved used literacy. For example, they used literacy in the form of naming, body language, and the use of representational symbols to convey their agency, thus accentuating that they had not been "broken" by the repressive and brutal system of slavery.

The enslaved also used *emancipatory literacies* to strategize means through which they could achieve liberation from slavery. The more common modes of becoming emancipated involved escape and insurrection. Examples of this use of literacy for the purpose of liberation can be seen in the slaves' utilization of quilting to map escape routes to freedom, as well as the secret literacy lessons provided by allies (black and white, enslaved and free) who clearly understood the grave consequences associated with exposure and their conscious decision that the realization of liberty and full equality were well worth the peril (Paul, 2016).

With the advent of Reconstruction (1863–1877), the demise of slavery, and the institution of the Freedman's Bureau in 1865, black schools (at all educational levels) were initiated. Although the black enslaved came to literacy late because of a government-sanctioned denial of literacy and educational opportunity, they nonetheless became literate.

Thus, it is essential that contemporary arguments regarding African Americans' putative lack of facility with Standard American English and literacy learning be considered in the same context in which other English Language Learners' struggles with language and literacy are viewed (Paul, 2016). It is of utmost importance to view any lags in language and literacy development attributed to African Americans as probable outcomes associated with the long-term, systemic, and government-authorized denial of Standard American and British English to enslaved Africans.

Further, such ahistorical and flawed arguments fail to acknowledge the tremendous strength and resilience demonstrated by black language and literacy learners, in addition to their noteworthy resistance efforts. When we permit narratives of black failure to go forth unchallenged, we grant our democracy permission to absolve itself from its collective responsibility to fairly and adequately address the needs of all citizens.

Now we shift focus to Native Americans, the other group (discussed in this chapter) for whom race played a key role in their education. Cautious estimates indicate that the New World was populated by three to five million indigenous people prior to 1492 when Columbus arrived. By 1850, however, there were approximately 250,000 Indians remaining (Bureau of the Census, 1993). This devolution of their numbers appeared to be primarily caused by the devastating American practices of conquest and colonization.

For many European settlers (including those who became the first American colonists), the Indians' emphasis on communalism and their belief in the interdependence of all living things stood in stark contrast to the values of rugged individualism and manifest destiny privileged by the more powerful invaders (Paul, 2017).

Yet after it was determined that the "Indian Problem" wouldn't be solved by decimation of the group (as it was mathematically impossible), the focus became assimilation and (as per usual) assimilation campaigns oftentimes concentrated on education. In relation to Native Americans, "annual congressional appropriations for Indian education rose from $75,000 in 1880 to nearly $3 million in 1900" (Adams, 1998, p. 3).

In addition, "in 1891 Congress declared that school attendance for Indian children should be compulsory. Two years later it added teeth to the measure by authorizing the Indian Bureau to 'withhold rations, clothing, and other annuities' from those parents who resisted sending their children to [government] school" (Adams, 1998, 3).

Shortly thereafter, the government intruded even more by establishing Indian Boarding Schools, in which large numbers of Native American children were snatched from their families for the purpose of accelerating the assimilation process and removing all traces of the children's Native American culture. Established in 1879, the first off-reservation boarding school for Indian children was the Carlisle Indian School in Carlisle, Pennsylvania.

By 1900, Congress had created a network of Indian schools composed of 147 reservation day schools, 81 reservation boarding schools, and 25 off-reservation boarding schools. Even more unfortunate was the fact that these Indian Boarding Schools were far too frequently breeding grounds for physical and psychological abuse of the students they were supposed to serve, as well as for pedophilia.

As stated by Tatum (1997), "Though the U.S. government's practice of removing children from their home environments was reversed in 1930, by then several generations of Indian children had lost their traditional cultural values and ways, and yet remained alienated from the dominant American culture" (p. 146).

So in consideration of this truly problematic racial history lived by both blacks and Native Americans in the United States, it is blatantly obvious that race has been and remains a factor in educating children of color. Yet to cast race as the sole or primary reason for failing city schools is limited and myopic. Such an explanation dismisses the strength of intersectional linkages between race, ethnicity, and class that have existed throughout American history.

CLASS AND URBAN SCHOOLING

There is a very long saga linking global schooling to economic theory. That tradition can be traced to analyses of education in tribal societies, as well as ancient China, Greece, Rome, and India (Collins, 1977). Within these contexts, formal education has been mythologized as an integral dimension of the struggle to provide students with "practical economic skills" that were believed to give them a leg up in securing and maintaining steady work (Collins, 1977, p. 5).

This early link between formal education provided in schools and the attainment of "practical economic skill[s]" is fragile, at best, and almost nonexistent, at worst. For example, in early tribal communities, most job-related skills were obtained through apprenticeships with skilled others who also happened to be family members in most instances (Collins, 1977). In the case of highly skilled workers like blacksmiths or shamans, apprenticeships were still the primary form of transferring occupational knowledge, but these apprenticeships were conducted in secret and away from the apprentice's family (Collins, 1977).

Education using apprenticeship as the primary mode of instruction continued as a prevailing educational practice and subsequently emerged prominently in literate societies like the Greco-Roman empire. So for the most part, formal schooling (that would be obtained in a physical school) was highly impractical and failed at its paramount task of preparing students for the workforce as many of its advocates claimed it did (Collins, 1977). By most accounts, the only practical skill taught in formal schools was literacy.

For the reasons cited, one would need to question the central claim that formal schools were designed to impart "practical economic skill" because they failed so miserably at this task. Thus, some (including the author) believe that imparting such skills was actually a very low-level priority that disguised education reformers' real goals, which were "cultural integration . . . prestige of particular associational groups, and . . . political control by and within formal organizations" (Collins, 1977, p. 5). Equally noteworthy, however, is that "actual reforms in schools have rarely matched such aspirations" (Tyack and Cuban, 1995, p. 1).

From its inception, formal schooling (no matter where it appeared throughout the world) seemed designed to reinforce socioeconomic fault lines more than anything else. While the United States has been less studied because of its status as a nascent nation, the earlier pattern regarding the seemingly planned impracticality of formal schooling and plausibly unconscious reinforcement of socioeconomic fault lines appeared to hold true here as well. To highlight an earlier point, these US-based economic explorations predate and outnumber those discussing the impact of race in schooling.

Many of the economics-related analyses of American schooling appear focused on the socioeconomic purposes and growth of public education. One of the most studied questions has been whether mass industrialization and immigration served as the primary catalysts for the proliferation of public schooling in urban centers. One of the most enduring myths surrounding the question is that both trends actually increased the demand for urban public schools.

Common, prevailing wisdom was that the heightened ascent of urban public schools was inextricably linked to the industrialization of cities and the amplified need for a skilled workforce. Bowles and Gintis (1976) conjectured that mid-nineteenth-century educational reforms like the growth of public education resulted from the influx of new groups into the American workforce and urban centers, as the bulk of the mass industrialization movement occurred in the nation's cities. Yet, again, it is important to note that (globally) schools didn't traditionally provide the type of practical skill needed for success in an industrialized workplace.

The crux of the Bowles and Gintis argument rests on the premise that this influx of industrialization and its new labor force demands prompted employers to more greatly support public schools. As per the theories, they viewed public education as the most efficient vehicle through which to socialize new workers, and that socialization process included assimilating them into American culture while concomitantly imposing social order and control (Meyer, Tyack, Nagel, and Gordon, 1979).

Further, the Bowles and Gintis argument seems to be conceptually grounded in *human capital theory*. Human capital theory is built on the premise that there must be a skilled and educated workforce as societies become industrialized. It is also supported by the inherent belief that the bulk of general schooling enhances a student's economic value to the society in which he or she lives (Friedman, 1962).

Human capital investments, as per human capital theory, are "precisely analogous to investment in machinery, buildings, or other forms of nonhuman capital. Its function is to raise the economic productivity of the human being" (Friedman, 1962, pp. 100–101).

Therefore, schools became more popular and necessary because they were believed to fulfill those functions and offer skill-based training (Field, 1976). According to Field (1976), "The increase in demand [led] to a rise in wages of educated workers, which produce[d], in turn, an increase in the incentive to invest in schooling, leading to greater enrollments and, in some instances, political pressure to socialize the costs of schooling" (p. 524).

In large part, however, it was again a myth that American public schools actually provided skill-based job training. Most in the skilled trades (like their counterparts throughout the world) learned their crafts through apprenticeships long prior to the inception of public schools and after as well. By most accounts, there were relatively few urban center jobs that required advanced skill in the nineteenth century. Those jobs were most often held by the children of the aristocracy, who predominantly attended private schools over the public schools designed for the masses (Field, 1976).

Yet while some education reformers based their entire argument regarding the increased strength of public schools on the human capital argument, others contended that it wasn't a foregone conclusion that industrialization naturally led to an increased need for an educated labor force. This assertion was evidenced by the fact that the growth of rural schools (during this same time frame) outpaced that of urban schools (Field, 1976).

In multiple studies of this period in Boston's history, for example, it was determined that the clear majority of industry jobs was unskilled and filled by children and recently arrived Irish immigrants (Field, 1976). This pattern also held in other cities, as many of the same types of new workers flocked to other urban centers like Philadelphia and New York. In fact, "the nation was awash with recent immigrants (accounting for about 80 percent of the population growth between 1820 and 1860)," making nativist sentiments politically popular (Walberg and Bast, 2003, p. 58).

Further, the vast majority of these newly arrived immigrants originated from Southern, Central, and Eastern Europe. Most were also Catholic and lacked a comprehensive understanding of "American" moral and ethical values (Field, 1976). Many were children as well. "Anti-Catholic sentiment led most states to amend their constitutions to restrict or prohibit government aid to private schools" that had heretofore been the predominant school providers for these children (Walberg and Bast, 2003, p. 59).

In response to that anti-Catholic bias, the number of Catholic schools proliferated and the schools took full ownership of Catholic children's spiritual development in those schools. Catholic school teachings necessarily countered the public schools' emphasis on the King James version of the Bible and the decidedly anti-Catholic information disseminated (Walberg and Bast, 2003).

Prior to 1890, the vast majority of Europeans migrating to North America originated from Northern and Western European countries like the United Kingdom, Germany, Sweden, and Switzerland (Banks, 1994). With the approach of the twentieth century, however, an authentic culture war began to brew, as new immigrants from Southern, Central, and Eastern Europe made their way to the United States. These new immigrants from Greece, Ireland, Italy, and Poland (to name a few) brought with them new customs, languages, and, most importantly, Catholicism.

SECOND WAVE US IMMIGRANTS AND PUBLIC EDUCATION

This new wave of immigrants posed an even greater challenge for public schooling and prompted struggles regarding its mission and purposes, in addition to whether or not public education could be considered truly egalitarian. As discussed earlier in the chapter, public schooling had always maintained a societal status quo regardless of whether that preservation was inadvertent or deliberate.

For all intents and purposes, the modern child was seen as a person who would ultimately learn to be a citizen and develop the potential to be a productive worker (Popkewitz, 1997). "The education of my child contributes to your welfare by promoting a stable and democratic society. . . . There is therefore a significant 'neighborhood effect'" (Friedman 1962, p. 86). But this was only true under the proper circumstances that seemed to include completely shutting the parents of immigrants out of that socialization process. Thus, the origins of "in loco parentis" took root.

In this particular instance, that socioeconomically driven preservation goal was consonant with sustaining an Anglo-Saxon way of life and the maintenance of existing socioeconomic hierarchies. As Friedman (1962) states, "The major problem in the United States in the nineteenth and early twentieth century was not to promote diversity but to create the core of common values essential to a stable society" (p. 96).

With that said, the "American school system, like other American institutions, embraced Anglo-conformity goals" (Banks, 1994, p. 21). Therefore, two of the public school system's major objectives toward that end included eradicating distinctively ethnic traits exhibited by these newly immigrated groups and coercing them into assuming Anglo-Saxon values and behaviors.

This assimilation process put forth white Anglo-Saxon Protestant culture as the standard bearer for other cultures to emulate. The process also necessitated that these newly arrived groups shed their distinctive cultural features by anglicizing their names and adopting English in an effort to gain full acceptance.

This view of schooling appears to be in concert with *structural reinforcement theory*. Structural reinforcement theory suggests that "the rise of mass public schooling represents the development of universal agency of socialization to take the place of other institutions whose efficacy has been impaired by economic transformation" (Field, 1976, p. 524). To better illustrate the point, John Stuart Mill stated that the development of affirmative moral attributes in public school students was *just as important* as the skill development required for the increased labor demands imposed by industrialization.

Classical economists, like Mill, whom many of his contemporaries blamed for the perversion of liberalism—taking it from a viewpoint that privileged private rights to a "mild form of socialism" (Boaz, 1997, p. 25)—emphasized strong linkages among education, religion, morality, and the maintenance and reinforcement of social order (Field, 1976). This position is a rather curious one for Mill, in particular, because he previously appeared to caution against government interference that involved the "infringement of liberty" (Boaz, 1997, p. 25).

Whereas human capital theory rested on the unrestricted market of goods and services, there was apparently no consideration of the socialization and assimilation processes (Field, 1976). With the latter structural reinforcement model, however, "order is a public good, the maintenance of which cannot be left to the market" (Field, 1976, p. 535).

So it appears that the structural reinforcement model also served as the foundation upon which the authorization of schools as assimilation agencies rested. In those instances where parents and families were deemed incapable of or unsuitable to initiate this morality-laden socialization process with their own children because they were either too poor, too "stupid," or too new to the country to be of much benefit, that responsibility was wrested away from them and the task of socializing their children fell almost entirely to the public schools, as did the inculcation of societally acceptable moral values.

For instance, the Boston School Committee made the following public statement in addressing the large number of Irish immigrant children who would potentially flood its municipal public school system during the early nineteenth century:

> Taking children at random from a great city, undisciplined, uninstructed, often with inveterate forwardness and obstinacy, and with the inherited stupidity of centuries of ignorant ancestors; forming them from animals into intellectual beings, and, so far as a school can do it, from intellectual beings into spiritual beings; giving to many their first appreciation of what is wise, what is true, what is lovely, and what is pure; and not merely their first impressions, but what may possibly be their only impressions. (Katz, 1971, p. 40)

In an expression of his support for the educational reform of kindergarten, US Commissioner of Education William T. Harris expressed similar sentiments in 1903:

> "The kindergarten is really essential for the salvation of the children of the slums, that is to say, the children of the three weakling classes of society." The offspring of these "weaklings"—the thriftless, the immoral and the unintelligent—can be redeemed by the "powerful system of nurture" of the kindergarten that teaches self-respect, perseverance, moral ideals, and industry. (Tyack and Cuban, 1995, p. 1)

For some, it makes little difference how beautifully worded and lofty the goals are cast in these statements, as that which emerges most clearly is the blatant disrespect for and abject dehumanization of these children and families for the sole reason that they weren't American-born and/or deemed ethnically acceptable.

Further, the quotes lay bare the increasingly heavy-handed role that government (in this instance, public schools) assumed and the almost complete governmental usurpation of parental authority, with a government agency seizing (in a legally protected way) the role of parents to determine and serve the best interest of their own children.

This schism regarding the role that education should fulfill also seemed to play itself out in respect to the content taught and curriculum introduced in the nation's public schools. By most accounts, we see the first indications of tracking and ability grouping around this time as well. That might hold little surprise for most; what is surprising, however, is that it was introduced by Progressives rather than Conservatives.

After all, it was Progressives who considered the schools (as then constituted) to be inherently unequal. It was Progressive educators who worked from the assumption that "offer[ing] different kinds of coursework to children with different ability levels, different backgrounds, and with different projected futures and career paths" was the most effective approach to schooling (Gamson, 2007, p. 181).

These Progressive reformers had a simple solution for all that ailed public schooling throughout the nation. That panacea involved widespread usage of new intelligence quotient testing and the proclamations made by one of the test originators, Lewis Terman, who was convinced that "measuring differences in student ability would lead to more efficient, effective schools" (Gamson, 2007, p. 180).

As Gamson (2007) explains, however, "Given the gift of hindsight, it is difficult to comprehend how progressive educators understood IQ testing as a democratic practice" (Gamson, 2007, p. 183), especially in consideration of the fact that many now view testing, tracking, and ability grouping to be inherently unequal and "thinly disguised vehicle[s] for social control and the perpetuation of the social order" (Gamson, 2007, p. 184).

Again, it is important to note that the proposed coursework distinctions were class based rather than racially discriminatory in nature. Again, the reason for its location as socioeconomically driven doesn't rest in the premise that racism and racial discrimination were nonexistent or hadn't previously manifested. Instead, it is specific to the fact that race as a consideration in schooling became a real and pressing issue post-1954 when *Brown v. Board of Education of Topeka* was won in the US Supreme Court.

There is yet another fascinating dimension to this argument regarding the economic roles and purposes of education in the United States, specific to the fact that it appeared to concomitantly play itself out in similar ways with another group of recent immigrants, newly emancipated slaves in the American South.

When speaking about immigrants and education, African Americans are oftentimes left out of this important discussion or their immigrant status is overlooked. Further, that status isn't customarily afforded the same degree of respect that is given to immigrants who chose to come to the United States rather than being made to come against their own volition. This omission is particularly unfortunate because rightfully considering the group as immigrants would add insightful nuances and make for a more accurate representation of the facts.

The United States could best be described as a "settler society, in which the ruling majority consists of immigrants from other societies. Members of this immigrant majority have come to improve their economic, political, and social status," according to late educational anthropologist John Ogbu (2003,

p. 49). Ogbu went on to state that, within a settler society, there are generally two types of minorities.

There were those who, although nonwhite, came and continue to come to the United States for similar aspirational reasons as the original white settlers. Then there was a second group who were forcibly made part of the US fabric "against their will, through colonization, conquest, or slavery" (Ogbu, 2003, p. 49). Obviously, African Americans were considered among the latter group. Like Native Americans, Alaskan Natives, original Mexicans, and Native Hawaiians, African Americans would fall into the category (named by Ogbu) as "involuntary or nonimmigrant minorities" (2003, p. 50).

SAME WINE, DIFFERENT BOTTLE... THE PURPOSES OF EDUCATION AND RECENTLY EMANCIPATED SLAVES FROM THE AMERICAN SOUTH

While many would cast the longstanding argument regarding the economic roles and purposes of education for newly emancipated slaves in the Reconstruction-era South as the *Washington-DuBois Debate* rather than the more widely referenced *Hampton-Tuskegee Idea*, its origins took root long before and actually predate plausible involvement from W. E. B. DuBois. In actuality, the Hampton model was inaugurated in 1868, the same year as DuBois's birth (Anderson, 1988).

Simply expressed, Booker T. Washington and his wealthy benefactor, Samuel Chapman Armstrong, put forth a model of education for recently emancipated slaves that, although initially intended to prepare teachers to staff the schools ex-slaves attended, became much better known for its emphasis on trade training and apprenticeships, instilling a strong work ethic, and privileging economic development within the black community.

As per Armstrong and Washington, economic freedom was envisioned as the only authentic mode through which black people would truly become free rather than continuing their dependency on white Southern planters for jobs as sharecroppers. For more progressive blacks, this plan represented a Faustian bargain with the white South because black Southerners were being asked to totally shun politics and redirect their attention to the less potent and previously untested waters of economic development (Anderson, 1988).

So while many cast the Hampton-Tuskegee Idea as a "great compromise" (p. 44), others were left wondering whether it was a true compromise or a ruse used to disguise black capitulation and acquiescence (Anderson, 1988). It was this skepticism and prevailing sense of dissatisfaction that spurred one of Washington's most potent adversaries, W. E. B. DuBois.

Without the right to vote and fully participate in the American political process, an emphasis on vocational training was pedestrian and ineffectual, according to W. E. B. DuBois and his contemporaries. In a stinging critique that appeared in DuBois's *The Souls of Black Folk* (1990), the intellectual takes Booker T. Washington to task for promoting an educational program that "practically accepts the alleged inferiority of the Negro races" and pointedly accuses Washington of asking black people to relinquish their "political power . . . insistence on civil rights . . . and the higher education of Negro youth" (p. 42).

According to DuBois (1990), Washington's focus on industrial education, amassing wealth, and the appeasement of the South had done little good and a great deal of harm, which resulted in the "disenfranchisement of the Negro; the legal creation of a distinct status of civil inferiority for the Negro; [and] the steady withdrawal of aid from institutions for the higher training of the Negro" (p. 43).

Chapter Two

The Emergence of Race in the Debate on Urban School Reform

To be diverse is to be unequal. (Gamson, 2007, p. 178)

As established in chapter 1 of *Unlearning Failure*, this book's central premise isn't that race played no role in past iterations of urban school reform. Instead, the book challenges the extent of the role that race actually played then and continues to play presently. Too many liberals rest their whole case for maintaining failing urban public schools and continuing to disserve urban families and communities of color on the big bad wolf of racism, contending that racial animus has been the sole driver with respect to funding and other disparities between urban, suburban, and rural school districts throughout the nation.

While in no way minimizing the historical impact of racism or the fact that there are legitimate instances of racism omnipresent even in contemporary society, that claim has become toothless and effete over time.

First of all, it is overused. Second, it has become synonymous with the squelching of dissent when strategically used to dismiss stronger and more viable arguments solely on the basis of the word's shock value. Third, racism (itself) is a very complex and sophisticated concept to unpack; therefore, it defies overly simplistic and oftentimes inaccurate liberal analyses, as well as hyperbolic attacks that use race as the centerpiece of otherwise anemic arguments.

This book submits that race might not have taken on that historical primacy in past explorations of urban school reform conducted during the late nineteenth and much of the twentieth centuries. From a social science standpoint, it would be nearly impossible to establish race as the leading causational factor in relation to the continued failure of urban public schools that may even be designed to continue failing.

For example, here is one indisputable fact. The sheer size of many urban schools contributes to their inability to well educate the students who attend them. There are a number of well-regarded education studies in which the findings are consistent and clearly identify smaller class sizes (typically viewed as fifteen to twenty students in a respective class) as "important determinant[s] of a variety of student outcomes, ranging from test scores to broader life outcomes. Smaller class sizes are particularly effective at raising achievement levels of low income and minority children" (Schanzenbach, 2014, p. i).

Overall, smaller class sizes have consistently been linked to elevated levels of student engagement, increased time spent on educational tasks, and broader opportunities for high-quality teachers to more effectively tailor instruction to meet the learning needs of the culturally diverse students they serve (Schanzenbach, 2014). In addition, teachers who reliably spent more time on educational tasks conversely spent less time on behavior modification and classroom management practices.

Another noteworthy point centers on the fact that debates regarding class size are longstanding. For instance, floating the reduction of class size as a viable school reform measure can be traced to 1850 or thereabout. At that time, however, different terms were used to address the same issue with "one room schools" and "graded and ungraded classrooms" appearing as the most popular verbiage (at that time) to address the same present-day crisis (Tyack and Cuban, 1995).

Nonetheless, there's also truth in the claim that uneven research bolsters assertions pertaining to the positive benefits of smaller class sizes, especially those putatively found in secondary schools. The skepticism surrounding the issue appeared to resurface with the 2013 publication of Malcolm Gladwell's *David and Goliath: Underdogs, Misfits, and the Art of Battling Giants*, in which he deemed research on smaller class size inconclusive and characterized it in the following fashion: "But the evidence suggests that the thing we are convinced is such a big advantage might not be such an advantage at all" (2013, p. 44).

While many education scholars have taken Gladwell to task regarding his unconventional conclusion for numerous reasons, others have questioned the argument's faulty premise as it is based upon a single research study and limited to his observations and scant research on the suburban Shepaug Valley Middle School in Connecticut. By most accounts, Shepaug Valley would be considered an outlier to the substantial body of research conducted over an equally impressive time frame on class size.

Although Shepaug Valley Middle School currently has a pupil-teacher ratio of 9:4:1 and employs approximately twenty-one teachers, Gladwell curiously shines a spotlight on the school as support for his argument that class size doesn't matter. He contends that the size of the school's fifth grade has varied over the course of twelve years (ranging from ten to twenty-three students) without any discernible change in the high achievement scores those students have customarily garnered. But this argument is a deceptive one, despite the fact that the deception is most likely unintentional.

The most pervasive impacts of supersized classes (and it is doubtful that anyone would identify the class sizes Gladwell reports at Shepaug Valley as such) are predominantly felt in urban centers, in addition to those school districts serving a majority of students of color and/or poor youngsters. In contrast, the most recent demographics for Shepaug Valley Middle School show that its student body is 90 percent white and 90 percent of its students are ineligible for free or reduced lunch.

Although the majority of research supporting the positive impact of smaller class sizes has been conducted in the elementary grades, it is admittedly difficult to extrapolate those findings and apply them to secondary schools in the preponderance of instances. First, most secondary school students receive departmentalized instruction for the bulk of the school day and travel to different classes throughout the day where each class might have a widely disparate class size (Jepsen, 2015).

Additionally, anyone who has taught secondary school (especially in urban centers) knows that the number of students appearing on the attendance roll frequently differs (greatly) from the number of students actually appearing in the class. Without a doubt, these factors would necessarily complicate a researcher's ability to get an accurate read of class size in middle or high school.

Usually, the most viable arguments with respect to disproving the benefits associated with smaller class size do so on the basis that class size can't be teased apart from other variables that might also positively impact student performance (one way or the other). Linked to that argument is the attendant one contending that the high costs associated with hiring more teachers to bring down class size outweigh the modest gains that might be accrued from it (Jepsen, 2015).

Still, the vast majority of class size research supports the premise that smaller class size (not to the exclusion of other factors) makes a positive difference in the schooling of low-income and minority students, most of whom attend school in urban centers. In fact, research suggests that the greater the size of the school youngsters attend, the more likely there will be an adverse impact on those students' standardized test performance.

So the fact that such a large number of urban schools continue to maintain large class sizes appears counterproductive to the academic success of the students attending them. Further, it seems to significantly contribute to the

Asian/white–black/Latino achievement gap and inadvertently perpetuates cycles of academic failure for urban school youngsters.

Therefore, despite criticism and questions about their efficacy, many charter schools that have set up shop in the same neighborhoods where these oversized public schools exist seem to achieve much better educational outcomes, in part due to their reduced class size.

The dilemma of inferior schooling in urban centers has been stubbornly persistent and commenced prior to the point that large numbers of students of color actually started attending them. In fact, these inferior urban schools have existed for close to two centuries now. This point is especially noteworthy in consideration of the fact that the vast majority of schools were lawfully segregated along lines of race prior to 1954. Thus, it stands to reason that other consequential variables added to the intransigence of the problem and extended beyond the singular dynamic of race.

Further, it can't be unequivocally stated that racism alone is the causal (rather than correlational) factor in this case or any other. Establishing causation is nearly impossible because of the potency of intersectionality, such as what exists between race and socioeconomic status. In most instances, intersectional linkages elevate the synergistic effect of factors that are independently strong.

Therefore, as race played an integral and consistent role in the history of the United States, it can be assumed to have played a comparable role in US urban school reform. But as highlighted in chapter 1, socioeconomic status appeared to play a far greater historical role than race did during the nineteenth and early twentieth centuries. By most accounts, race seemed to prominently enter the debate on urban school reform with the back-to-back rulings on *Brown v. Board of Education of Topeka*.

In respect to the national consciousness, race (as it pertained to schooling and school reform) seemingly didn't become a consequential focus until the first *Brown v. Board of Education of Topeka* ruling in 1954. The reason is grounded in the fact that US schools were largely segregated prior to that point, with many Northern and Southern states appearing to unquestioningly accept the segregated status of their schools with some states even privileging the practice.

Additional emphasis needs to be placed on the fact that, while the segregation challenges of Arkansas, Alabama, and Mississippi are well documented and well known, similar and equally pernicious battles played themselves out in New York, California, New Jersey, and Massachusetts.

THE UNREALIZED PROMISE OF *BROWN*

On May 17, 1954, a unanimous Supreme Court handed down the landmark *Brown v. Board of Education of Topeka* ruling, the first of two rulings that would comprise the *Brown* decision. The *Brown* case served as the culminating suit in a series of school desegregation cases spanning approximately a century. Yet *Brown*'s legal remedy differed sharply from its predecessors.

In the prior cases, redress for those claims (based on the segregated public schools' inferior quality and the subordinated educational value they provided to students with no other viable alternative except to attend them) was composed of imperceptible and unenforceable court orders solely requiring that the facilities be made equal and nothing more. Needless to say, there was often no resulting change and the status quo was reinforced; thus, the segregation persisted (Bell, 2005a).

Another detail that often appears to be forgotten or excluded for some reason when the topics of *Brown* or school desegregation arise is particular to the fact that not all of the earlier desegregation litigation was filed on behalf of black plaintiffs. To forget or attempt in some way to minimize the value of the noteworthy and highly successful efforts undertaken by Mexican American parents on behalf of their children is quite simply wrong.

For example, there was *Independent School District v. Salvatierra*, effectively proving that a Texas school district discriminated against Mexican children on the basis of race, and the 1931 *Alvarez v. Lemon Grove*, upending school segregation in California by solidly establishing that separate educational facilities for Mexican children actually retarded their English language development skills, in addition to proving counterproductive to those efforts geared toward Americanizing them (Donato, 1997).

"Of course, the legal referent for *Brown* is the 1896 *Plessy v. Ferguson* case that *Brown* reversed" (Ladson-Billings, 2004, p. 4). The *Plessy v. Ferguson* case, in which African American plaintiff Homer Plessy challenged the existing segregation laws by riding in a train car designated for whites only, was upheld in court via a court decree stating that segregation could be legally supported as long as the black facilities were equal to those for whites.

This ruling and others like it were often quixotic to most independent and objective observers, however, because mere sight confirmed that the facilities could in no way be considered equal upon even the most rudimentary of inspections.

Although Plessy's legal challenge was based on his claim that his Fourteenth Amendment guarantee to equal protection under the law had been violated, the court ultimately decided that no such breach had occurred. Fifty-eight years later, that landmark decision was reversed by another such landmark case, *Brown*, and it was decreed in 1954 that "separate educational facilities are inherently unequal."

Further, the concept of racial segregation itself does (in fact) violate the Constitution's equal protection clause. "The equal protection clause clearly bars racial segregation because segregation harms blacks and benefits whites in ways too numerous and obvious to require citation" (Bell, 2005a, p. 34). The success of that legal argument, which used the equal protection clause as its foundation, then led other cultural groups (that is, special education parents and women) to adopt it as well—and yes, it worked just as effectively for them.

While the legal precedent established under *Brown v. Board of Education of Topeka* was groundbreaking and symbolically unparalleled, thought has evolved over time in a rather unpredictable way on the matter. In hindsight, it has been cast as more of a Pyrrhic victory than a real one, resulting in very little tangible educational and/or school-based reform.

Indisputably, *Brown*'s indirect impact was momentous and largely responsible for social change that included "thrusting the desegregation issue onto the national agenda, searing the conscience of previously indifferent northern whites, providing legitimacy to desegregation demands by blacks, or inspiring (especially southern blacks) to challenge the status quo" (Klarman, 1994, p. 81). Yet in the final analysis, acknowledgment is wide and common that *Brown*'s direct impact on school desegregation was severely limited and its indirect contribution to racial change overstated (Klarman, 1994).

In similarly pessimistic terms, brilliant legal scholar Derrick Bell (2005a) contended the following regarding the impact of the *Brown* decisions:

> The remedies set forth in the major school cases following Brown—balancing the student and teacher populations by race in each school, eliminating one-race schools, redrawing school attendance lines, and transporting students to achieve racial balance—have not in themselves guaranteed black children better schooling than they received in the pre-*Brown* era. Such racial balance measures have often altered the racial appearance of dual school systems without eliminating racial discrimination. (p. 37)

Again, agreement on this point appears broad and, in some instances, seems to come from rather unlikely sources. For example, renowned multicultural education scholar Gloria Ladson-Billings struck a parallel chord on the matter of *Brown*. She stated that "the results of the *Brown v. Board of Education* decision of 1954 represent a kind of landing on the wrong note. Brown's intentions were good and honorable. Its fight was just, but from a 2004 perspective, one might argue that we landed on a wrong note" (2004, p. 3).

Another meritorious criticism of *Brown* is specific to the Court's myopic focus on addressing inequities particular to school funding and academic programming over demanding that the states actually desegregated their schools in an enduring way. "Because the commitment of the courts has been to create schools that are more equitable solely in terms of dollars and programs, segregation has gone unchecked" (Orfield, Ee, and Coughlan, 2017, p. 6).

The Bell and Ladson-Billings quotes, in particular, serve as important segues to the next criterion that has been used in evaluating *Brown*'s real impact: its longevity. In that respect as well, change has been largely fleeting, with contemporary US schools presently more segregated than they were at the point of Martin Luther King Jr.'s assassination.

This de facto resegregation quite naturally occurred and is explicitly linked to the residential segregation that continues to exist throughout the nation. "Housing segregation plays a major role in shaping the landscape of school segregation" (Orfield, Ee, and Coughlan, 2017, p. 15). Thus, the cycle of school segregation continues as there was never truly a substantive abatement of the problem (Orfield, Ee, and Coughlan, 2017).

The failings of *Brown* are also easily traceable to two key factors. One, its real-time, tangible implementation was slow and/or near nonexistent (in many states) because SCOTUS (Supreme Court of the United States) had no true power to actually enforce its own judgments.

For example, in 1955 and within the context of the second *Brown* ruling, SCOTUS "rejected the NAACP request for a general order requiring desegregation in all school districts, issued the famous 'all deliberate speed' mandate, and returned the matter to the district courts" (Bell, 2005b, p. 100). At that point, it became readily apparent that most school districts opted against voluntary compliance with *Brown*, instead choosing to retain counsel and resist compliance until they could resist no more (Bell, 2005b).

That legendary clause citing that the implementation of *Brown* should be carried out with "all due deliberate speed" was principally a throwaway phrase because it subtly implied that it was permissible for school districts to move at a snail's pace with school desegregation or, even better, to do nothing at all to advance the effort (Brown, 2004). In tandem, Congress's approach was just as noncommittal. It also failed to send a positive signal to the district courts to proceed with implementation in a serious way until 1964 with the passage of the 1964 Civil Rights Act (Brown, 2004).

Regarding the many impacted school districts throughout the nation, the clear majority opted for a similar minimalist approach when left to their own devices to enforce SCOTUS's *Brown* judgments. That constrained approach to implementation ultimately resulted in a de facto reinforcement of the formally sanctioned segregation of the past.

For instance, St. Louis, Missouri, sought to enforce the ruling and desegregate its schools using a tripartite system. Its Board of Education issued a directive advising school administrators to proceed in such a manner as to call for "a minimum number of boundary changes in order to relocate the smallest possible number of pupils" (Rist, 1973, p. 33).

As established earlier, school segregation is reinforced by residential segregation. Therefore, the decision of the St. Louis public school system virtually rendered the *Brown* decision null and void in the city of St. Louis. Further, within the context of his report to the US Commission on Civil Rights in 1967, Semmel (1967) noted that approximately 90 percent of all black elementary school students still attended racially segregated black schools post-*Brown* (Rist, 1973).

The second factor weakening the promise and potential of the *Brown* decisions to make transformative social change was the formidable backlash they provoked from the South. Singlehandedly, the *Brown* decisions elevated race over class as well as compelled many Southern whites who weren't necessarily fixated on race to become so, especially as the issue was so polarizing that it forced them to side with their fellow Southerners on an issue they felt had the potential to remove the last vestiges of power they had left (Klarman, 1994).

While race might have been a tangential issue for this particular group, it wasn't the primary one. Somewhere along the way, the desegregation issue had substantially morphed into one of "federal compulsion versus states' rights" (Klarman, 1994, p. 98). To illustrate the contrast, the following consideration should be made.

Pre-*Brown* (during the late 1940s and early 1950s), there had been a tidal wave of state and local antidiscrimination legislation enacted. The vast majority that was promulgated focused on fair employment practices and open public accommodations, although some actually forbade racial segregation in public schools (Klarman, 1994). Additionally, the late 1940s brought a perceptible rise in the number of black candidates running for public office in many cities of the upper South, with some even occasionally winning (Klarman, 1994).

Another example of the racial moderation that existed prior to *Brown* included the political victories of Big Jim Folsom of Alabama. Folsom

> won resounding victories in Alabama's Democratic gubernatorial primaries in 1946 and 1954 on populist platforms of higher state spending on schools, roads, and old-age pensions, as well as abolition of the poll tax and reapportionment of the state legislature. Folsom's posture toward blacks was one of genuine fraternity, invoking their right to a fair share of Alabama's wealth, speaking of "fellowship and brotherly love," and disparaging racial divisions on the grounds that "all men are just alike." (Klarman, 1994, p. 88)

Post-*Brown*, however, the most appalling manifestation of the racial backlash incited by the court rulings was the racial violence that appeared to skyrocket, including a dramatic rise in the number of lynchings. The issue also became a bellwether test for those who decided to foray into politics and, in the short term, resulted in the elections of quite a number of politicians who had publicly committed to preserving the racial status quo that was in place pre-*Brown* (Klarman, 1994).

Yet without a doubt, it is a mistake to characterize all resistance to *Brown* as "racist" and emblematic of white supremacy. Whether we're discussing the issue of school desegregation or any other caustically polarizing phenomenon around the topic of race, there is a tendency among some to oversimplify and/or cast the debate in narrowly moralistic and condemnatory terms as a fight between those who are "racist" and those who aren't. Herein lies the problem. The point is moot that racial animus played and continues to play a significant role in US history. Just as dead is the point that racism infiltrated our public schools by extension.

The fact that racial animus has historically permeated the very soul of the United States is a given. No, that isn't an acquiescence; it is an established fact. Whether its causes have been predicated on shaky justifications for the institution of slavery; misreading the Bible, US Constitution, and attendant documents; junk science upholding the mortally flawed concept of white supremacy and racial inferiority for people of color; or an irrational and unattainable standard of "racial purity," racial animus is intricately interwoven into the fabric of America.

There is no authentic and measurable way of knowing what motivated any of the opponents to desegregation, unless that motivation was expressly revealed by them and/or their statements/actions were codified or memorialized in some way. Further, it is exceedingly difficult to determine people's motivations without direct evidence, and it is even more difficult in instances in which the actors are dead. We are often left to speculation in such cases, and hopefully we can all agree that speculation is inexact.

In this particular instance, a highly compelling argument could be made that the steadily increasing encroachment of the federal government's power drove resistance efforts to *Brown*, especially as the decisions came at a great cost to the states' independence and decisively eroded their constitutionally derived rights. The pain associated with the erosion understandably intensified because it came fresh on the heels of the South's loss of the Civil War.

Traditionally, federalism was viewed as the ideal set forth in the US Constitution and a benefit to the republic. It is defined as follows: "both the national government and the smaller political subdivisions [in this instance, the states] have the power to make laws and both have a certain level of autonomy from each other" (Legal Information Institute, February 7, 2018). The principle of federalism is reified in the Constitution's Amendment X, stating that the powers not delegated to the United States by the Constitution, nor prohibited by it to the States, are reserved to the States respectively, or to the people.

The US public education system had operated under this federalist tradition from its inception, with powerful control belonging to the local and state governments and a co-equal strength for the federal government being discouraged (Kaestle, 2007). There is healthy debate on the point at which that power balance shifted, with some contending it was immediately after World War II and others associating the pendulum swing with *Brown*.

For those who associate the shift to World War II, the plausible reason for the link is specific to the GI Bill and its impact on postsecondary education for veterans. With the GI Bill, "each veteran who qualified was given a maximum sum per year that could be spent at any institution of his choice, provided it met certain minimum standards" (Friedman, 2002, p. 90). The dramatic departure here is particular to the fact that this funding came directly from the federal government.

By most accounts, however, the unprecedented intervention of the Supreme Court, as well as the civil rights legislation that followed, prompted the vast majority to posit that (in reality) the *Brown* decisions represented the most sizable shift in federal power, actually surpassing the changes that resulted post–World War II. Yet, as mentioned throughout this chapter, while SCOTUS had no power to actually enforce its rulings on the matter, the Civil Rights Act of 1964 was able to successfully coerce states into compliance.

THE CIVIL RIGHTS ACT OF 1964 AS THE MOST POWERFUL ENFORCER OF *BROWN*

An important acknowledgment rests on the point that the Civil Rights Act of 1964 was not the first civil rights bill to be enacted in the contemporary United States, although it is undoubtedly much stronger than its predecessor, the Civil Rights Act of 1957. The Civil Rights Act of 1957, the first civil rights bill promulgated since Reconstruction, had a difficult path to enactment.

While it was eventually passed, much of its original language had been stripped away following a filibuster from South Carolina senator Strom Thurmond (Aiken, Salmon, and Hanges, 2013). In fact, Thurmond concluded a twenty-four-hour, eighteen-minute-long filibuster invective on August 29, 1957, that was solely designed to stall passage of the bill as he didn't have the votes required to outright kill it.

Also, in its later and bulked-up iteration, the Civil Rights Act of 1964 served as a highly effective vehicle through which to force the hand of those states that had refused to voluntarily comply with *Brown*. "Only after the 1964 Civil Rights Act threatened to cut off federal educational funding for segregated school districts and the Department of Health, Education and Welfare [HEW] . . . adopted stringent enforcement guidelines, did the percentage of southern black children attending public school with whites rise to 6.1 percent in 1965–1966, 32.0 percent in 1968–1969, and 91.3 percent in 1972–1973" (Klarman, 2004, p. 84).

Using the Elementary and Secondary Education Act of 1965 (ESEA) that was part of the 1965 civil rights legislation as the primary conduit for change, there was increased federal spending on public education and a new way to punish those states choosing to resist school desegregation. Ultimately, the recalcitrant Southern states found resistance to school desegregation no longer economically sustainable as it resulted in the substantial loss of federal funding.

The change in the states' calculus was specific to the fact that their desegregation efforts had now become a condition for receipt of federal funding (Klarman, 2004). Further, "the 1964 Act also gave the U.S. Secretary of Education the authority to collect data to document implementation of Brown and provide grants to school districts to assist with school desegregation efforts" (Brown, 2004, p. 182).

Unfortunately, even the threat to withhold federal funding wasn't as powerful as the sheer will of ordinary white parents across the nation, who decided that they would do what their local and state governments could no longer do. Personally, they would defy the compliance orders by simply moving out of district and to areas that remained predominantly white, thus keeping the decisions about their children's educational fates in their own hands and outright rejecting intervention from the federal government that included SCOTUS.

Chapter Three

The Infusion of Big, Federal Cash ... Throwing Good Money after Bad

> There is nothing that the federal government can't ruin with good intentions and unintended consequences.
> —Bob Taschler, Friend and Bergen County Republican Activist

> Nothing lasts longer than a temporary government program.
> —Ronald Reagan

The preceding chapter of *Unlearning Failure* concluded with an introduction of the Civil Rights Act of 1964 (CRA). The context was specific to its use as a means of forcing compliance on those schools that continued to resist enforcement of the *Brown* rulings. In that chapter as well, a most fitting description of the Civil Rights Act was proffered. It was described and seen by many as the single most powerful tool the federal government had with respect to dealing with recalcitrant school districts and forcing their figurative hand regarding the actual implementation of *Brown* rather than the mere and worthless promise to implement that had been given thus far.

The law's potency came from the newly derived powers it gave to the US Attorney General to initiate litigation on behalf of black plaintiffs in thousands of school districts across the nation that persisted in running illegal, racially segregated public schools (Brown, 2004). Further, the new law fully empowered the US Secretary of Health Education and Welfare (HEW) to start data collection efforts that would document implementation of *Brown* or lack thereof, as well as provide school districts with federally funded grants to assist them with their desegregation efforts (Brown, 2004).

The most important point regarding these newly configured data collection capabilities, however, is the fact that the data collected provided the aforementioned plaintiffs in school desegregation cases with concrete evidence of the offending school districts' failure to enforce school desegregation plans (Brown, 2004). Last, the federal government (via the CRA) assumed all of the associated legal costs for trials, all the way up to the US Supreme Court. So there's little surprise in the fact that, within four years, the US Department of Justice had successfully brought hundreds of these desegregation cases to a close.

Yet this chapter picks up where the preceding one left off and examines the strength of subsequent and costlier federal interventions that impacted public education, generally, and seem to have exacerbated the urban public school crisis, in particular. For example, whereas the CRA specifically helped to alleviate persistent racial disparities that had not been corrected post-*Brown*, the Elementary and Secondary Education Act of 1965 (ESEA) was much more expansive and much less targeted to achieve pragmatic and realizable goals.

SPENDING OTHER PEOPLE'S MONEY TO FUND YOUR CONCEPTION OF A MORE SOCIALLY JUST WORLD

The ESEA, considered one of the hallmarks of the Great Society legislation, was enacted on April 11, 1965, and touted for ensuring that the national interest in equal access to quality education for all American school children was satisfied. It served as one of the signature pieces of legislation passed under the Johnson administration with former US Department of Health Education and Welfare head John W. Gardner playing a key role in shepherding the bill through the process and to fruition. Subsequently, HEW became and remains the US Department of Education.

Initially, ESEA funding was awarded by formula-driven block grants to states and municipalities that agreed to minimally adhere to HEW's exceedingly lenient program and spending guidelines. In fact, most US federal funding flows to its subnational governments in a similar way, via large formula grants like those for Medicaid, Temporary Assistance to Needy Families (TANF), highway planning, and construction (Manna and Ryan, 2011).

Yet ESEA was distinctive from the other programs with respect to the almost total absence of legislative oversight, as well as the virtually nonexistent accounting required from grant recipients for their spending and/or the educational outcomes achieved by their Title I students. "Legislative ambiguities in ESEA coupled with minimal congressional oversight led to abuses of ESEA funds, including provision of general aid funds to all students instead of targeted resources for the special needs of educationally disadvantaged students" (Thomas and Brady, 2016, pp. 52–53).

Emphasis must be placed on the fact that the aforementioned leniency didn't lead to just mild abuses of the system. No, it led to systemic and massive abuses as well as extreme cases of fiscal mismanagement. As has become standard operating procedure with the vast majority of federally funded programming, very little of the monies earmarked for the express purpose of improving the quality of life for disadvantaged Americans actually makes its way to those Americans. Therein lies the problem.

Instead, corruption, graft, and waste become pervasive and the money quickly disappears. It is for this reason that most contemporary Fiscal Conservatives (including the author) are so anti–federal programming. Back to ESEA, however, as "millions of dollars appropriated by the Congress to help educationally deprived children [were] wasted, diverted or otherwise misused by State and local school authorities" (Martin and McClure, 1969, p. i).

As the monies were initially fungible, municipalities and states had broad discretion in the ways in which they saw fit to use this new pot of free money. Yet most of us are well aware that the tab for a free lunch is always picked up by someone. In this case, it was picked up by the average taxpayer of federal taxes. Here is a segue to another criticism of ESEA and, by extension, Title I funding.

One of the more common criticisms of Title I was leveled by Progressives and centered on the claim that its implementation process failed to appropriately incorporate input from parents and community members whose children benefitted (or failed to benefit) from the law. While the sentiment motivating the statement and intent behind it are well understood and well-intentioned, the criticism itself is illogical.

If the children were benefitting from a program designed to eradicate poverty, what is the likelihood that their parents and community members weren't also poor? So that leads to the next question. Being identified as poor and qualifying for antipoverty federal funding, what is the likelihood that these families actually paid federal taxes instead of being the beneficiaries of those taxes? The answer is they probably didn't. So why should their input have been more valuable or even equal to those who paid the bill for such governmental benevolence?

Yet even with such far-reaching discretion as provided under the ESEA/Title I program and spending guidelines, it is difficult to decipher how some of these purchases could have been justified. For instance, Title I funding was utilized in the construction of two lagoons for sewage disposal in Attala County, Mississippi; the purchase of five school buses in Indianapolis, Indiana; and renovations on a county-owned television studio in Fresno County, California (Martin and McClure, 1969).

Additionally, Title I was improperly used to supplement the salaries and travel budgets of school administrators in Alabama when the positions and travel weren't explicitly linked to Title I or fulfilling the educational needs of

Title I students in the majority of cases. The funds were expended to construct additional classrooms at six schools in Columbus, Ohio; to purchase football uniforms in Macon County, Alabama, and band uniforms in Oxford, Mississippi; and to buy eighteen portable swimming pools in Memphis, Tennessee (Martin and McClure, 1969).

Further, a point of clarification is in order here. Thus far, the examples provided demonstrating misappropriation of Title I funding are clear. The truth is plain and unadorned, as the offending school districts and administrators certainly should have known that they were potentially abusing the ESEA funding guidelines with these outrageous purchases and acquisitions.

Straining credulity, however, they represent only a small fraction of the total misuse of funds. US Department of Health Education and Welfare audits suggest that about 15 percent of Title I funding had been misappropriated at that time (Thomas and Brady, 2016). As was more frequently the case, the vast majority of school districts and administrators were simply confused by the federal government's lack of clarity on allowable expenditures.

During the early years of implementation, in particular, the federal government adopted a "hands-off" style of enforcement unless outright malfeasance was detected. Yet it appears as if the federal government's "hands-off" policy remained firmly intact even when outright abuse was identified. Unfortunately, this laxity in direction and enforcement paved the way for literally hundreds of interpretations of the statute and a vast array of implementation strategies, many of them imperfect and deeply flawed.

While the bill's original intent remains admirable, the ESEA (like many other well-intentioned federal programs) has quite regrettably devolved "into a hodgepodge" (Rotherman, 1999, p. 4) over time. Since the ESEA's inception in 1965, numerous titles and programs were added. Some of those titles included the Bilingual Act (Title VII), the Women's Educational Equity Act (Title IX), and the Improvement of Educational Opportunities for Indian Students Act (Title X).

Almost a score ago, the ESEA was aptly described as a "14-title federal law that . . . directs more than $13 billion in annual education assistance to states and school districts through a crazy quilt of more than 50 programs. The largest and best-known program is Title I, which is the cornerstone of the federal government's commitment to ensure educational equity for poor children" (Rotherman, 1999, p. 1).

Late philosopher, theologian, and critic of most modern Western cultural institutions Ivan Illich described Title I as the "most expensive compensatory program ever attempted anywhere in education" (1971, p. 5). He went on to note that "between 1965 and 1968 over three billion dollars were spent in U.S. schools to offset the disadvantages of about six million children" (1971,

p. 5). Yet in the end, there was no discernible, evidence-based improvement in the disadvantaged students' educational outcomes (Illich, 1971).

Illich's 1971 pronouncements continue to apply and remain relevant today more than fifty-four years and substantially billions of dollars later. Despite the passage of time or the extraordinary amounts of cash dumped into making ESEA/Title I functional, the achievement gap between low-income and middle-class students as well as the intransigent gap between students who are Asian/white and black/Hispanic remain firmly ensconced and disconcertingly wide.

Even more unfortunate is the fact that the ESEA's underlying philosophical framework and methods of implementation remain largely intact all these years later, without any direct evidence of enduring repurposing or reconceptualization. In fact, the ESEA continues to be currently arranged and administered in pretty much the same way it was in 1965, predicated on the same philosophy.

For example, the US Department of Education continues to choose against conducting needed audits or scrutinizing audit systems that are not properly working. This persistent lack of sufficient Title I enforcement by the US Department of Education has seriously hindered the comprehensive implementation of the program (Havard, 2009).

Additionally, these enforcement difficulties and perpetual noncompliance with the statutory mandate have been well substantiated by the US General Accounting Office (now the Government Accountability Office) in its 2002 report titled *Title I Funding: Poor Children Benefit through Funding per Poor Child Differs*. The report confirmed that the US Department of Education failed to properly monitor accountability and assessment requirements of Title I. Therefore, it was identified as a grave and telling flaw in the statute's efficacy.

Aside from clearly identifying the USDOE's lax enforcement, the report more importantly made recommendations that would figuratively "right the ship." They included suggestions for additional audit training, bulked-up oversight roles for the states, and a heightened degree of attention devoted to monitoring fiscal requirements (Havard, 2009).

Still, all these years later, Rotherman's 1999 quote remains highly applicable when he describes federal education funding sent to subnational governments as "a Byzantine patchwork of programs and formulas targeting discrete needs and populations. This creates confusion, redundancy and inefficiencies. It also makes systematic collection of useful data a herculean and thus far unsuccessful task" (Rotherman, 1999, p. 4).

The ESEA and its attendant Title I might be noteworthy for another consequential reason as well. It is highly possible that the overreaching, gargantuan law served as the starting point to a whimsical train of thought based on the shaky premise that throwing federal money at a social problem—without emphasis on accountability or fiscal monitoring in most instances—would magically end in compelling results.

Now, some scholars contend that this phenomenon of throwing taxpayer funding at social problems didn't commence with liberals as commonly accepted. For example, Tyack and Cuban (1995) contend that, while it has been widely asserted that liberals like to throw money at educational problems, the percentage of per pupil expenditures rose most dramatically during the politically conservative decades of the 1920s and 1950s rather than the liberal 1960s.

On its face, however, such a claim is problematic. First of all, it isn't an apples-to-apples comparison. Second, the dollar amount that could have potentially been spent during either the 1920s or the 1950s starkly pales in comparison to the more than $130 billion spent to date on a program that was supposed to be temporary by most accounts.

ESEA: COMPROMISE LEGISLATION OR THROW-UP-YOUR-HANDS CONCESSION?

So how did such a mortally flawed bill as the ESEA even make its way out of committee, let alone become law? Anyone even minimally familiar with the legislative process knows that rarely does the original bill see the light of day or will the best one (qualitatively) move forward to passage. In most instances, it is a deeply flawed and imperfect compromise version of the original bill or bills that is enacted. Usually, it's the one that leaves the least amount of blood on the table at the end of the negotiation process. That was certainly the case with the ESEA.

The ESEA of 1965 gained passage by Congress after considerable compromise. With Title I being the law's most prominent feature, the funding initiatives attached paved the way for an even greater level of governmental intrusion into the affairs of local and state governments than they had previously experienced with either *Brown* or CRA. This pill was an especially bitter one for the South to swallow on the heels of multiple losses (including the Civil War and the Goldwater defeat), in addition to what they properly considered a rapidly encroaching and unwelcome federalism.

As a result of the fact that Title I's funding mechanism was a very effective way to force some degree of compliance and for the federal government to exercise control over an area that had historically remained the purview of the states (Havard, 2009), many would consider the South's concerns as prescient and a sign of what was to come with respect to increasing the size, scope, and power of the federal government, with states and municipalities ceding more of their own authority to the behemoth in Washington, DC.

Other entities that have historically opposed federal intervention into the public schools included the National Catholic Welfare Council (NCWC), the domestic policy arm of the Roman Catholic Church. The council traditionally stood in staunch opposition to any federal aid for education, and their reasoning was twofold and legitimate. First, the organization opposed the federal regulation of education. Second, they vehemently disagreed with the premise that federal aid predominantly went to and continues to go to public schools over private ones (Kaestle, 2007).

Eventually, the NCWC softened its hardline stance on federal education aid. But this more pliable position came only after the federal government sweetened the education assistance pot by incorporating transportation services and access to school nurses into existing federal education aid packets, in addition to making aid for those services available to private and parochial schools.

Yet lest some readers begin to think that the opposition to ESEA and federal aid to education (generally) came exclusively from Conservatives, they should be mindful that the ESEA's most vocal critic was the labor union the National Education Association (NEA). Its primary objection centered on the disbursement of *any* federal funding to private and parochial schools (Thomas and Brady, 2016).

So the ESEA symbolized a compromise legislation of sorts between those who were totally opposed to federalism in any form and those who were concerned about expanding the educational horizons of poor black and Mexican youngsters. In order to arrive at a consensus and achieve bill passage, the federal government had actually been forbidden from substantive intervention in local Title I expenditures (Havard, 2009). "The initial Title I funding scheme was in effect two dimensional, as evidenced in the legislation—it provided federal funding and did not disturb basic educational infrastructure" (Havard, 2009, pp. 129–30).

Now, while it is absolutely true that the ESEA and its attendant Title I could be aptly described as bad legislation for all of the many reasons delineated heretofore, it would be unfair to imply that legislators and laypeople alike paid little attention to the severe difficulties inherent and made no attempt to remediate those vast and sundry problems.

For example, in response to widespread reports of misused Title I funding (most particularly, the 1969 Martin and McClure bombshell report *Title I of ESEA: Is It Helping Poor Children?* cited earlier in this chapter), President Richard M. Nixon signed legislation in 1970 that added safeguard protections that would potentially ensure against continued misapplication of Title I aid.

It appeared to President Nixon that one of the most commonly abused features of the law was particular to the manner in which many subnational governments were using Title I funds as a stopgap accounting measure when their local and state education budgets had been expended for a particular year. "As a result, many of the expenditures paid for goods and services that previously had been purchased with state and local monies" (Havard, 2009, p. 132).

The original intent was that Title I funds were expressly designated for supplementing state and local education aid that would be used to provide academic services for poor students. In too many instances, however, those funds were being improperly used to supplant rather than supplement subnational education budgets. This deep concern that Title I funds were replacing education aid that had already been expended rather than enhancing the ability of local school systems and states to provide supplementary educational services led to much tighter regulation (Havard, 2009, p. 132).

Another problem that had been identified regarding Title I expenditures was particular to some school districts remaining invested in fighting lost battles from the past. So these noncompliant school districts persisted in the illegal practice of underfunding schools that maintained predominantly minority and poor student populations. As a result, the president added two new provisions that would increase the heft of the admittedly weak ESEA and Title I law.

The first new requisite established that the federal aid derived from ESEA and Title I was earmarked for the express purpose of "supplement[ing] not supplant[ing]" money spent by the states and municipalities on public education. The second mandated that Title I schools receive state and local aid that is "comparable to that received by other schools in the state" (Robelen, 2005, p. 2).

While it is readily apparent that President Nixon was the first to take on the problems associated with the ailing ESEA/Title I, he wasn't the last. In fact, every president following President Lyndon B. Johnson made some effort to "fix" the broken law. For example, President Jimmy Carter introduced a provision permitting Title I to be utilized schoolwide in the event that 75 percent of the children attending were eligible for the funds. Yet that seems to be the extent of his contribution. So in the interest of time and space, the discussion that follows will only focus on those presidential efforts that were the most radical or innovative.

TRANSFORMING ESEA/TITLE I

The next consequential modification to ESEA/Title I came sixteen years after the law's initial passage and during the Reagan administration. Specifically, President Reagan, intent on making good on his campaign promise to reduce the federal government's size, ushered in a significant reduction of federal education funding, in addition to reducing big government's imprint in all domestic policy areas, chiefly public education (Thomas and Brady, 2016).

During 1981—the first year of his administration—the Education Consolidation and Improvement Act (ECIA) was passed. It was a feature of President Reagan's more expansive Omnibus Budget Reconciliation Act (OBRA) that actually did reduce federal funding across most domestic policy areas. Under OBRA, Title I of ESEA was renamed Chapter 1.

Although the newly titled Chapter 1 of ESEA retained its original legislative intent of funding compensatory services for educationally disadvantaged students, significant reductions in federal aid and relaxed regulatory requirements led to fewer eligible students actually being serviced (Thomas and Brady, 2016). Further, the consolidation resulted in the reduction of regulatory and paperwork requirements for states and local school districts (Robelen, 2005).

President Clinton assumed office in 1993 and reauthorized ESEA in 1994 by signing the Improving America's Schools Act (IASA) into law. The reauthorization required states to develop standards and align those standards with assessments for all students. Another noteworthy and interesting point here is that, while many mistakenly attribute the concept of "adequate yearly progress" (AYP) to President George W. Bush and the No Child Left Behind Act, President Clinton was actually the concept originator.

He was the first president to declare that school districts nationwide were obligated by law to develop identification systems for those schools failing to make AYP, as well as to design viable improvement plans. There is general agreement, however, that President Clinton's version of AYP is much looser and more forgiving a version than President Bush's 2001 model, especially regarding the definition of AYP and the imposition of consequences on those schools that failed to meet the standard (Robelen, 2005).

President Clinton's proposal was momentous in another way as well. It represented a seismic shift toward performance-based funding and stricter accountability for states and local school districts (Rotherham, 1999). Nonetheless, despite the consistent and steady attention devoted to fixing the law and the enhancements implemented, there remained "wide variance in the degree to which states . . . complied with the requirements of the new Title I" (Rotherham, 1999, p. 1).

Yet no prior overhaul of ESEA has been grander in scale or more scrutinized than the No Child Left Behind Act of 2001 (NCLBA) signed into law by President George W. Bush in 2002. NCLBA is remarkable for myriad reasons. Most markedly, it expanded the ESEA's testing requisites and instituted a highly aggressive federal posture with respect to holding states and school districts accountable for demonstrating improved student performance using standard metrics.

NCLBA mandated testing of all students in reading, math, and science throughout grades 3 through 8 and once in high school. States were also obligated to annually assess school progress and identify those schools that were making AYP, as well as those that failed to do so. In the event that a school received Chapter 1 aid while failing to make AYP, it became susceptible to the imposition of federally defined improvement measures, and those sanctions intensified if a school was identified as struggling over the course of several consecutive years.

To President Bush's credit, but also drawing considerable consternation that very few understood, NCLBA also required that all public school classrooms have "highly qualified" teachers teaching in them (Robelen, 2005). The introduction of this new mandate came on the heels of many urban public school apologists contending that, while numerous variables contributed to the low quality of education students received in these schools, one of the most significant was linked to the paucity of highly qualified teachers who taught in them.

Thus, NCLBA addressed the criticism and started to require that school districts hire "highly qualified" teachers for all academic subjects. In translation, all teachers were required to possess a bachelor's degree, hold full state certification, and be able to demonstrate an appropriate level of content area knowledge in the subjects they taught (Manna and Ryan, 2011).

Nonetheless, despite NCLBA's aggressive stance regarding the implementation of the law and the highly prescriptive approach used to remediate schools failing to satisfy AYP benchmarks, large loopholes in the reauthorized law remained and those ambiguities diminished state and local enforcement capabilities (Manna and Ryan, 2011).

This diminished capacity was also exacerbated by USDOE reticence to truly hold states and subsidiary school districts accountable because they simply didn't have the necessary tools to monitor implementation or supervise grant administration at those levels (Manna and Ryan, 2011). "Federal education officials were at times unable to keep up with the amount of oversight work and technical assistance required during implementation. That limited the department's ability to hold states to the law's requirements" (Manna and Ryan, 2011, p. 525).

There's another reason that NCLBA makes for a fascinating case study of sorts. Prior to this point in history, the most disturbing problems associated with the law had been lax fiscal accountability from the states and local school districts, in addition to too many subnational governments appearing virtually incapable of producing evidence-based, result-oriented student achievement outcomes that justified the large amounts of federal aid they expended.

With NCLBA, however, the focus on these past bad actors dulled considerably as a new set of bad actors emerged. These new bad actors came predominantly from the private sector and saw textbook/educational materials sales and test construction as the next big profit vista. Clearly, they were invested in seeing NCLBA succeed. But rather than viewing it as a way to ameliorate educational opportunities for America's children, they saw it as an opportunity to increase their respective sales margins. So for the first time in contemporary America, an education law ushered in a new era of crony capitalism and the corporatization of public schools.

For example, Harold McGraw III, CEO of McGraw-Hill and a member of President George W. Bush's transition team, reported a steady increase in profits for shareholders since 2001 and directly attributed that sales growth to the No Child Left Behind Act (Edelsky and Bomer, 2005).

Noted literacy education scholar Richard Allington characterized the reports serving as the basis for NCLBA's Reading First guidelines (that had been promulgated by the National Reading Panel [NRP]) as much more entrepreneurial than research based. In fact, he identified them as "entrepreneurial (as in buy stuff) masquerading as research summaries" (Allington, 2013, p. 521).

So let's take a step back at this point. The NCLBA was accompanied by corresponding Reading First guidelines, which were entirely focused on early literacy and gave primacy to direct and explicit literacy instruction for beginning readers. That early literacy intervention focused primarily on phonemic awareness, phonics, and fluency. In essence, "the Reading First guidelines . . . turned the use of explicit, systematic phonics instruction into law (Altwerger, 2005, p. 4).

Yet alarmingly, there appeared to be strong and intricate relationship webs between the false claims inherent to the NRP report, evidence-based literacy researchers, and those researchers' lucrative involvement in their own entrepreneurial ventures, while concomitantly profiting from friendly connections to the Bush White House (Garan, 2005).

Still, there was an even more shocking fundamental problem with the research that went into informing NCLBA federal education policy. Subsequent to its active involvement in changing the literacy instruction landscape of the American primary grades, the Reading First Program was deemed entrepreneurially corrupt and ineffective (Allington, 2013), thus compelling Congress to defund it. Yet that disbandment didn't come prior to the point that more than $4 billion had been expended (Teale, Paciga, and Hoffman, 2007).

So once again, there appeared to be no accountability or oversight demonstrated with regard to federally funded education expenditures underwritten by the federal government. This time, however, the culprits weren't states and local school districts to which the American people had grown accustomed. This time, the culprit was more specious and ugly. Big business had been given a wide berth to make money at the expense of our children.

In this particular instance, there wasn't even the pretense that an underlying compassion and concern for children motivated its actions, especially in consideration of the fact that business's primary motivation is to make money and that's exactly what it did under the protection and auspices of the Bush White House and perpetually flawed education policy.

Now, one of the NCLBA fixes to most easily win the distinction as the most creative and dangerous belongs to President Barack H. Obama. The distinction of being the most creative is specific to the way the president and his Secretary of Education Arne Duncan got buy-in from states and local school districts to adopt the Common Core State Standards (CCSS).

Despite protestations to the contrary from President Obama and Duncan, states were compelled to adopt the CCSS in order to qualify for Race to the Top (RTTT) grant funding. That coercion resulted in fifty-one states indicating support for the CCSS, with only Virginia, Texas, Nebraska, and Alaska never moving forward with implementation.

RTTT, the brainchild of President Obama, was a "$4.35 billion, competitive, voluntary grant program offered to the states and funded through the $787 billion American Recovery and Reinvestment Act" (Onosko, 2011, p. 1). Another noteworthy point here is specific to the fact that the scale of federal investment in RTTT was unparalleled by any standard (Hershberg and Robertson-Kraft, 2009).

Additionally, the president and his USDOE head introduced a number of other practices and mechanisms that had previously been considered anathema in education circles. For example, in order to compete for RTTT grants, states had to demonstrate that they had incorporated changes that would make both their student assessment and teacher evaluation systems more rigorous.

Both of these newly configured systems would then be used to inform personnel actions like tenure, career development, and compensation. Now, while no RTTT application could be put forth for consideration without approval from the state's teacher unions, that approval amounted to little more than checking the figurative box.

Yet an even bigger point of contention between the president and teacher unions emerged. This one was particular to his embracing stance on charter schools. He clearly identified them as a crucial aspect of any school district's turnaround plan. Therefore, they needed to be well integrated into any RTTT grant application if that application was to warrant serious consideration. Needless to say, this stance intensified an already adversarial relationship between the parties.

The reason that President Obama's approach might be considered the most dangerous NCLBA fix is specific to the threat it posed to long-existing state and local autonomy. Now, the chapter has already well established that the autonomy was far from perfect. But rather than continue to tinker with it as past presidents had, President Obama decided to blow the system up.

The president believed that another reason that urban schools, in particular, were failing was linked to the fact that the students in those schools weren't learning the same content as students in highly successful school districts. There is any number of educators who could identify a top-ten list of reasons for this discrepancy, but it is highly doubtful that the lack of national standards would have appeared on anyone's list. The president, however, truly believed that there was a need for a national curriculum and set of standards (known thereafter as Common Core State Standards [CCSS]). For the president, CCSS implementation ensured that all students learned the same thing.

Many prominent education scholars have taken the president to task regarding this train of thought. They have properly cast the CCSS as a solution in search of a problem. Many have refuted the claim that we didn't possess a sufficient number of standards in the past or that our curriculum hasn't been as rigorous as needed. In fact, the contrarian argument would be that having high academic standards in place has very little to do with having students who are well equipped with the tools required to learn those standards.

Regarding curricular vigor, there are many educators who would contend that there's simply too much content stuffed into existing curricula and not enough time in the academic year to teach it, especially as some school districts consider "teaching to the test" to be the only legitimate content and what is most beneficial to students.

Most importantly, for the vast majority of education scholars who are conversant in the US Constitution, their biggest criticism rests on the point that CCSS masquerade as law when they were never enacted through Congress. Any attempt to nationalize the US school curriculum breeches the US Constitution and federal law, thus making the CCSS violative of Amendment X of the US Constitution.

SO WHAT'S THE CONCLUSION?

Sadly, despite the billions of dollars invested and the attention given by each and every president since President Lyndon Baines Johnson signed ESEA into law, its longstanding difficulties have persisted. Chiefly, these problems are specific to lack of legislative oversight and misappropriated funding.

As outlined in this chapter, there has been little abatement in either problem over the past fifty-four years. For instance, in the past decade and in spite of tighter regulations and efforts to rein in unwise spending, Chapter 1 funding was still used to construct two Olympic-sized swimming pools for poor children in Claiborne Parish, Louisiana (L. Lewis, 2016).

Therefore, this chapter concludes on a rather depressing note. Our best intentions have failed, and we must now face facts. The educational outcomes achieved have not been a good return on investment for the more than $130 billion invested in public education to date (especially for students who are poor and of color). As a result of this continued cycle of failure, it has come time for us to chart a different course.

This book's title *Unlearning Failure* puts forth its central premise. Is it even possible to *unlearn failure*? The author submits to you that it is not. Failure cannot be unlearned, but it can be dismantled. So again, we must chart a new course, and that course must be laser focused on children first . . . all children, including those stuck in failing urban schools.

It is time for us (especially those who claim to care about the least of these in our society) to actually live up to the ideals we espouse and no longer accept the substandard education these students have received for far too long. It should be wholly unacceptable to us to allow the destiny and life chances of one more urban generation to be solely determined by the quality of education they have received. The time is now to act and, in the process, to explore all the educational alternatives available to us.

Part II

Can Urban Schools Be Transformed in the New Millennium?

Chapter Four

Can Failure Be Unlearned?

Can Urban Schools Actually Be Transformed in the New Millennium?

> Failure is the word used most frequently to describe urban public schools in the United States, because the lists of problems confronting these institutions is so long and daunting. Low test scores, low grades, high drop-out rates, poor attendance, and generally unmotivated students usually top the lists of failings. Burned out and ineffective teachers who care more about protecting their jobs than helping students, typically follow complaints about students. Those more intimately familiar with conditions in urban districts point to dilapidated and unsafe buildings, administrations hopelessly mired in politicized and inefficient bureaucracies, and an endless series of reforms that never seem to lead to genuine improvement. (Noguera, 2003, p. 3)

This book's title poses two central questions that drive its scholarly exploration. First, is it possible to *unlearn failure*? Second, *can urban schools actually be transformed in the new millennium*? One of this book's major premises centers on the fact that those who support consistently failing schools are incapable of unlearning failure for it is, quite simply, too ingrained and now functions as a new normal for them.

Over time, failure has become comfortable and acceptable, especially as they aren't the ones most negatively and directly impacted by it. Those most vulnerable and highly susceptible, the students attending and their families, have been most harmed by the longitudinal effects of this toxic schooling.

Although it obviously isn't working for the students trapped within them and left with relatively few educational alternatives, the pervasive and long-standing failure of urban schools is apparently working quite well for some. It is working well for those who are invested in sustaining them despite their glaring lack of return on investment, paltry educational outcomes, and solid evidence that they ill prepare the majority of students attending them for successful, productive lives.

UNIONS STANDING IN THE WAY OF PROGRESS REGARDING URBAN SCHOOL REFORM?

Chief among those invested in maintaining the status quo would likely be American teacher unions, in which membership is primarily divided between the dominant sister unions the National Education Association (NEA) and the American Federation of Teachers (AFT). Now, unlike some previous books written on educational reform that have sought to assign blame for a majority of US public school ills almost exclusively to the unions, this book takes a more measured and nuanced tone, especially when it comes to discussing teacher unions' complicity in the persistent pattern of failure witnessed in urban schools.

That tone is derived from the author's direct working knowledge of teacher unions that comes from her past experience as a high-ranking elected leader in one of these unions. During the approximately eight years that she served in various elected capacities, the author was committed to protecting members' rights and fighting for fair contracts. During that time as well, the vast majority of the rank-and-file members she encountered were (to their credit) greatly interested in their students and highly dedicated to their professions. It was truly an honor to serve them.

Conversely, in the upper echelons of union leadership, she witnessed unequivocal fraud, corruption, and a propensity for using membership dues for questionable purposes, as well as an uncomfortably symbiotic relationship with the Democratic Party. So while *Unlearning Failure* will refrain from doing the customary hatchet job on teacher unions because of the author's immense respect for the rank-and-file members she served, the book will take a decisive and clear-eyed approach to identifying teacher union misdeeds.

Let's start from the basic premise that all unions have the potential for good. As such, there will be no categorical condemnation of them in *Unlearning Failure*. For instance, based on a single witness account and without due process, a septuagenarian New Jersey professor faced possible suspension with no pay a week and a half before Christmas.

There was also a rumor circulating that his department was systematically weeding out all professors who were of retirement age, and evidence appearing to tangentially support that claim surfaced as well. The union successfully beat back the suspension and there was no harsh penalty imposed. The professor was able to retire after a year or two of modified assignment.

There were also a large number of instances during which teacher unions have been able to secure commonsense gains for their members. For example, many children, civil union partners, and spouses of New Jersey public college/university employees had been previously ineligible to receive any tuition break from the respective institutions of higher education where their parents, partners, and spouses worked, even if those family members had been working at said college/university for a protracted period of time.

Further, there was a real and legitimate need here. Most employees' children, partners, and spouses are ineligible for generous financial aid packages because their incomes were too high. For the purposes of this discussion, guaranteed student loans (for which the repayment schedules and interest rates equate to little more than a federally sanctioned practice of usury) will not be included as viable sources of financial aid, especially given the fact that students can be stuck paying the interest on those loans into their sunset years.

It was the union that was able to eventually secure a 40 percent tuition reduction for the children, civil union partners, and spouses of these employees. While 40 percent is admittedly a modest reduction, it is a reduction nonetheless and does make a marked difference when student tuition bills roll around.

Since their inception, however, there's also been a mythology of sorts surrounding unions' principled origins and efficacy that has positively enveloped them. For example, American labor unions have taken credit for everything from the introduction of the weekend to paid family leave. While it would be disingenuous to state that they haven't secured many of these gains for their members, exception should be taken about the exaggerated nature of the claims regarding both their laudable beginnings and the level of success attained.

Despite the tall tale woven, "labor unions did not arise out of compassion for those who were ill-paid or unemployed. Rather, they emerged from the less noble motive of better-paid elites to keep the ill-paid and unemployed from entering their trades and driving down their wages" (Walberg and Bast, 2003, pp. 129–30). In addition, there are many who no longer see unions as effective, as evidenced by their plummeting participation rates. During the 1950s, participation in labor unions was at approximately 35 percent. Conversely, those figures for 2017 steeply dropped to 10.7 percent (Bureau of Labor Statistics, 2018).

Now, with that said and an acknowledgment that unions can and do serve the public good comes the attendant belief that association with a union should be strictly voluntary. Thus, if an employee is displeased with the efforts of her/his local union affiliate, fails to see the benefit of belonging to a union, or simply makes a dollars-and-cents determination that she/he can't afford any additional payroll deduction, that employee's First Amendment right should be honored and she/he shouldn't be compelled by law or otherwise coerced to pay agency shop fees.

Although the agency shop fees vary according to the union with which one is affiliated, some associated aspects can be considered standard. For instance, it is a safe bet to state that agency shop members pay almost full freight. By design, there is only a small difference (percentage wise) that distinguishes an agency shop payer from a full dues-paying one. The rationale here is that a big difference would serve as a disincentive for employees considering full dues-paying status.

As anticipated and in consideration of the US labor movement's tenuous health at the present time as well as the likely union-unfavorable *Janus* decision pending in the Supreme Court, there are some union supporters who will counter that employees making such a choice shouldn't be permitted to benefit from the union's efforts, including contract negotiations and/or the garnering of union protections.

Just for clarification, *Janus v. AFSCME* challenges labor unions' legal right to collect fees from agency shop payers for the service of collective bargaining. The case was argued before the Supreme Court on February 26, 2018, and a judgment is presently awaited. Here is some additional background on the case. In 1977, unions had been granted the right to collect agency shop fees, but the changing composition of the Supreme Court and doubts about the law's constitutionality have led to its revisiting (National Constitution Center, 2018).

This almost nonsensical "solution" proffered by some, wherein the union would selectively advocate for some members and not others, is a deeply flawed and troubling one. First, it is nearly impossible to achieve. After all, is there truly a neat and tidy way to split the bargaining unit and advocate for some and not others? Undoubtedly, all members will inadvertently benefit from any effort that is deemed to protect the union's common good.

In addition, these supporters choose to ignore the fact that the union already discriminates. It is an existing practice rather than a future threat. Presently and quietly, most unions distinguish between the representation afforded full dues-paying members versus those who are designated agency shop payers. The representation received by former union officials who left the union on bad terms is even worse. Just ask the author for verification of that fact.

Although unions frequently put on a good public face and visibly attest to the fact that they do not discriminate, most of those with intimate familiarity with them know that the nondiscrimination assertion is nothing more than a lie. Last on this point, the proposal to selectively represent employees violates the very principles undergirding trade unionism that include solidarity, strength in numbers, and fair representation regardless of status.

Yet there is a central point in this discussion of teacher unions that is germane to the chapter's broader context with respect to the continued downward slide of the nation's urban public schools. That point is specific to the defined role and responsibility of teacher unions, and it is also one that shouldn't be overlooked.

Although their public relation arms do a masterful job of convincing the American public that teacher unions are motivated by a love for and commitment to schoolchildren and young people, make no mistake about it. Their primary commitment is actually to their members, and that allegiance is manifested through the maintenance of an optimal number of jobs for those members, protection of their rights, and the procurement of bulked-up benefits packages even when they come at the expense of the states' fiscal health.

In recent times, there have been multiple instances in which municipalities have been bankrupted, left on the verge of bankruptcy, or their city-wide debt obligations have gone unmet because the respective governments simply couldn't afford to pay for the worker health and pension packages that had been negotiated. These cities include Prichard, Alabama; Compton, California; Detroit, Michigan; Pontiac, Michigan; Irvington, New Jersey; and Providence, Rhode Island, to name a few.

Honest brokers will readily admit that the downside of teacher unions' rock-solid devotion to their members comes at the expense of the very students they publicly profess to love. So while there is no suggestion of intentional malice on the part of the nation's teacher unions, there is a firm belief in the premise that "many of the policies that teachers' unions promote show utter disregard for the needs of students in general and low-income minority students in particular—not because unions don't care about kids, but because they care more about their members" (Riley, 2014, p. 97).

This commitment to their membership has also prompted teacher unions to fight sensible school closure plans for failing urban schools and seemingly obstruct all reforms that demand any kind of enhanced teacher accountability. For instance, New York City's local affiliate of AFT (the UFT) filed lawsuits to keep Harlem's historically failing schools open and, in 2012, Chicago teachers went on strike. Although they had a list of other grievances, the primary focus of the job action was the implementation of a new teacher evaluation system.

The proposed modification would have added a 40 percent weight to a teacher's ability to help students improve on annual standardized exams (Jeffrey, 2012). Further, it memorialized that new gauge as an integral component of their yearly performance evaluations (Jeffrey, 2012). In prior years, Chicago public schools' teacher evaluations took the form of an unsophisticated and unscientific checklist.

It is easily comprehensible that teachers might balk at being held accountable for factors that are beyond their control, and those variables can include students' maternal level of education, socioeconomic status, and the size of the school they attend, all of which play far more consequential roles in regard to students' performance on standardized tests than the teacher's role. Yet fighting against any and all forms of accountability is a totally different matter.

While it is understandable that teachers would argue that less weight be assigned to student performance on standardized tests as those scores pertain to their own evaluations for the earlier referenced reasons, balking about being held accountable at all strains credulity. There isn't a single profession that isn't required to adhere to some kind of industry standards and face consequences in the event that the profession consistently fails to satisfy those standards.

Thus, the desire to be absolved of total responsibility for the product one helped to produce (in this instance, competently prepared students who are capable of sustained academic and lifelong success) is anomalous and illogical. There isn't a single American industry without built-in quality controls. Further, it is a given that major restructuring occurs if that industry demonstrates an intransigent pattern of repeated failure.

The two cited examples will, hopefully, better illustrate the almost single-minded focus of teacher unions to protect member jobs and resist change or (in other words) be obstructionist. It is extremely unfortunate that this protectionism continues unabated, even in the face of compelling evidence that it is harming the very people teachers are supposedly responsible for helping.

Regrettably, their robust efforts to keep failing schools open for business (the vast majority of which have been struggling for decades if not centuries) perpetuate a seemingly never-ending cycle of generational harm in communities of color. Further, those efforts relegate the children of these communities to futures oftentimes replete with poverty, incarceration, and out-of-wedlock births that—in most instances—perpetuate the poverty cycle.

Of course, there will be readers of this book who might plausibly find its discussion of the ways in which organizational self-interests can cultivate the maintenance and propping up of dangerously ineffective urban school systems as harsh and hyperbolic. Yet others will wholeheartedly agree with the central premise. They will fully understand that the supposition is predicated on the psychological principle that people do not engage in any behavior (even a negative one) if there isn't some sort of payoff for them.

As a society, we have worked to address the urban school crisis for approximately two hundred years, and the results of that hefty investment of time, money, and thought have been middling to poor. In the following section of this chapter, a snapshot of the educational outcomes of some of the nation's largest contemporary urban public school districts will be discussed.

A STATUS REPORT ON URBAN PUBLIC SCHOOLS

Since approximately 1990, the National Assessment of Educational Progress has annually disseminated a *Nation's Report Card*. Within the context of these highly detailed reports, the National Assessment of Educational Progress monitors the scholastic achievement of US students on standardized tests. Those scores are comprehensively broken down into the following categories: *results for the nation*; *results for the states/jurisdictions*; and *trial urban districts* (NAEP, 2017a).

According to the 2012 *Nation's Report Card*, 79 percent of Chicago eighth graders couldn't read at grade level and 80 percent failed to attain a rate of basic proficiency in grade-level math. Here's another way to interpret those statistics. They reflect the fact that a mere 19 percent of Chicago eighth graders were deemed proficient in reading while another 2 percent were identified as advanced, leaving a grand total of only 21 percent scoring as proficient or better (Jeffrey, 2012; NAEP, 2017b).

On the eighth-grade math component of that test, a mere 17 percent of Chicago eighth graders scored proficient and 3 percent demonstrated advanced level aptitude. Thus, there was a 20 percent rate of students scoring at the level of proficient or advanced skill on the standardized math tests administered (Jeffrey, 2012; NAEP, 2017b).

Next up is Detroit. The lack of academic progress made by the Detroit public school system is epic in scale, as the district earned the 2015 distinction of scoring lowest among similar big city districts on math and reading four consecutive times (Lewis, 2015a). Specifically, the district underperformed during 2009, 2011, 2013, and 2015. According to the National Assessment of Educational Progress's *Trial Urban District Assessment (TUDA)*, fourth- and eighth-grade Detroit public school students fared worse than students in twenty other large urban districts (NAEP, 2017b).

Further, recent NAEP data suggest that there was no discernible improvement made for Detroit public school students in 2017 either. During 2017, the district hit a new low as its students scored worse than their counterparts in twenty-six other large urban districts (NAEP, 2017b). That damning criticism is only slightly blunted by the fact that *TUDA* included twenty-two participating urban districts in 2015 and an additional five districts joined in 2017. Again, however, this isn't good news for Detroit public schools. Even without the five new districts, DPS still performed worse than it did in 2015.

The NAEP initiated *TUDA* in 2002 with six participating urban school districts and it focused exclusively on the voluntary reporting of NAEP reading and writing assessments. In 2009, there were twelve districts added, and the NAEP assessment reporting included mathematics, reading, and science. Twenty-one participated in 2011 and 2013, twenty-two participated in 2015, and twenty-seven urban school districts partook in 2017 (NCES, 2017b).

Other facts about *TUDA* include the following. Unlike the *Nation's Report Card* that appears to be disseminated annually, the *TUDA* data seem to be collected biennially. That two-year window proves valuable because it offers additional time to gather more comprehensive and qualitatively better data. Yet in an effort to further nuance the Detroit public school system's scores as well as maintain balance and fairness, the *TUDA* scores should be viewed against a broader backdrop and within their proper context.

A 2017 Brookings Institution study found that academic failure wasn't relegated to Detroit alone. Instead, it was pervasive statewide. A pattern had been established with Michigan students habitually making the least progress nationally since 2003 (Lewis, 2015b). According to the study's author and University of Michigan professor Brian A. Jacob, Michigan made "the bottom 10 list on all four measures, and [ranked] dead last in terms of proficiency growth since 2003" (Lewis, 2015b).

The last city that will be highlighted in this section is Baltimore. As with Detroit, Baltimore's scores will be explored against a more expansive backdrop. Thus, in regard to urban school districts generally, the 2015 *Nation's Report Card* confirmed that urban school districts' collective rates of student achievement were unremarkable and dramatically low across the board. Their scores were distinguishable only in respect to the fact that they fell far below both state and national averages in the subject areas of math and reading.

Yet there were rays of hope, as evidenced by noted exceptions including Boston, Cleveland, Chicago, Dallas, the District of Columbia, and Miami-Dade County, all of which demonstrated substantial *Report Card* progress (Camera, 2015b). Further, several cities reversed course with respect to previous *Report Card* declines. Each of those cities came closer to meeting the national averages that had previously escaped them in at least one grade or subject (Camera, 2015b).

Baltimore, however, was omitted from the list of districts making considerable progress; it should be added that the omission was from a list on which the district had appeared on more than a single occasion in the recent past. Further, this exclusion came after Maryland won $250 million in Race to the Top (RTTT) funding. Maryland also saw the steepest test score drops (Camera, 2015a). In fact, "the average reading score for fourth-graders in Baltimore dropped 15 points since 2013; for eighth-graders, the average dropped 13 points. In math, students in grade four and grade eight each scored 19 fewer points than they did in 2013" (Camera, 2015b).

So while there were definitely pockets of sunshine with respect to the way urban school districts performed on standardized test measures, the overall forecast for them wasn't rosy. Herein lies the finely detailed nuance of *Unlearning Failure*. In the context of this book, there is absolutely no contention that all urban schools are failures and ill serve students, especially as current and solid evidence to the contrary exists, with some urban school districts making steady and strong progress.

Instead, *Unlearning Failure* makes a much more precise point. That point centers on the fact that there are far too many urban schools that can be characterized as failing, with sound proof substantiating those representations. Quite frankly, they've been permitted to fail for far too long. Once again, those who have been most harmed by the contemporary state of these schools are also those forced to attend them because (in many instances) no viable educational alternatives have been proffered.

In other instances, those invested in maintaining these failing schools have misled students and their families to believe that any truly liberatory option they might explore other than continuing to attend and prop up these horrible schools is a threat to democracy and life as they know it. That deceptive and intellectually dishonest argument evokes fear, and we all know that fear creates a type of mental disequilibrium that potentially paralyzes.

Now, whenever the topic of radically reforming urban public schools arises, we can expect the usual chorus of voices to emerge. Their questions typically include: *What does it say about us, as a society, if we give in to defeat and shut the doors of our public schools? If we decimate public schools in urban centers, what will happen to those students? What happens to those urban school students for whom vouchers and charter schools aren't options?*

For many, the hyperbolic nature of the concerns raised by urban school defenders is irritating for a host of reasons. First, there is no all-or-nothing proposition that has been put on the table for consideration. There is no conceivable way to shutter all of the failing urban schools in the public education system. There are simply too many of them. Further, such a proposal is laughable because the vast majority of public schools aren't failing. The vast majority of public schools are producing students who can read, write, and successfully complete mathematical computations.

That isn't the case, however, for the urban center schools discussed in this chapter. Here, we have grand-scale failure, and we have simply run out of turnaround options. Also, please note that the defenders' questions (listed earlier) are artfully worded and lean toward the melodramatic side.

In the history of American education, there's never been a grand-scale effort to dismantle public schools or decimate public education in urban centers. Yet with that statement comes an attendant reality that some choose to disregard. We already lost the battle of well educating most students in urban centers long ago. Just as with America's War on Drugs, we have seemingly lost the battle for the hearts, minds, and potential of the vast majority of students relegated to and trapped in failing urban schools.

Those students are confined to neighborhood schools that no longer effectively serve them. Time and again, the schools have proven themselves incapable of fulfilling even their most basic charge and academic mission, which is—first and foremost—to well educate children and young people who have no other option than to attend their designated neighborhood schools, despite the fact that those schools have failed for decades.

It appears that a primary reason for urban public school failure might center on the fact that there are no material consequences for that failure. "Schools can raise spending and reduce the quality of their service without fear of losing customers because they compete only in highly attenuated ways for students or funding" (Walberg and Bast, 2003, p. 98). Further, despite inefficiency, fiscal irresponsibility, and/or failure to produce tangible results, their doors stay open.

> The whole system is guided neither by efficiency or equity. The democratic impulse of school board members to win reelection, and administrators and teachers to retain their jobs and increase their salaries through collective and political actions, are not linked to the products they produce—children's education. (Witte, 2000, p. 201)

On an even greater scale, many of the students "dis-educated" in these schools end up failing at life because they've been so clumsily prepared to lead successful and prosperous ones. "Dis-education" is the "experience of pervasive, persistent, and disproportionate underachievement [of Black and Hispanic students] in comparison with their White [and Asian] counterparts" (Carruthers, 1994, p. 45).

The fact that these schools "dis-educate" rather than "educate" has led to the authorial decision to cast this debate as one particular to "urban school reform" rather than "urban educational reform." It is this author's contention that very little that purports to be education goes on within the halls of too many urban schools to count. Thus, referencing "educational reform" would serve as a misnomer.

Another thought centers on the point that, because these school failures do not impact the preponderance of American students, some of us are able to simply ignore their unsuitability for the populations they *are* charged with serving. Without a doubt, students attending these modern-day failure factories do not receive the best education that we—as a society—can offer them. Instead, the ZIP codes in which they reside dictate the quality of education they get. *Real Talk!*

The dilemma of subpar schooling (that is the rule rather than the exception in urban centers throughout the United States) continues unchecked and unrestricted because the vast majority of American schoolchildren aren't exposed to them. Yet here is an attendant issue that deserves thought and deliberation as well.

Although "decent" people don't express the thought in public, our societal actions convey our collective and misguided belief that these young people are getting the education they rightfully deserve. This belief is undergirded by the tremendously flawed myth of American meritocracy that mistakenly equates poverty with personal failing. It hints at the fact that poverty simply isn't consonant with American values.

If speaking clandestinely and given the assurance that their comments wouldn't be publicly attributed to them, some of these "decent" people might even feel comfortable enough to share their firmly held belief that students are trapped in these schools because their parents/caregivers don't work, expect handouts, and (least palatable of all) care less about their children.

All of these beliefs are shameful, as at no point in the history of this country has the amount of money a parent had dictated that parent's love and concern for her/his child. But they do reinforce one point. Specifically, they highlight the lack of collective willingness to fix urban schools. At one end of the spectrum, ready excuses are made for them, and at the opposite end, they're being declared beyond repair or redemption. Infrequently, however, are workable solutions or substantive remediation plans offered.

Now, not all motivations behind this reluctance to help are so cold-hearted and dispassionate. Some are quite sensible and reasonable. For instance, there are those who legitimately point to the huge dollar amounts of federal funding that have already been expended to bring urban schools up to par, as discussed in chapter 3. Unfortunately, those infusions of federal cash haven't resulted in a level of success that is commensurate with the investment made.

In addition, when one calculates the amount of school aid (local, state, and federal) that's subjected to graft, waste, and corruption or simply fails to make its way into urban center classrooms for the benefit of students, there should be little surprise regarding the lack of solid support for these schools. It should also be anticipated that legitimate questions will arise and expectations for continued funding and additional resources will dissipate as well.

There are still others whose lack of support for urban public schools is solely based on the inability of these schools to satisfy even the most basic, developmentally appropriate student benchmarks and related school progress indicators. For this group of detractors, the schools don't demonstrate consistent and reliable progress that is also easily documentable. So in the end, the investment of resources is far too great when contrasted with the meager returns received.

For example, according to the *Reading First Guidance Draft*, "by effectively teaching children to read well by the end of the third grade, we ensure that all students advance later to grades well prepared to achieve their full academic potential" (US Department of Education, 2002, p. 1). This emphasis on early intervention and teaching students to read by third grade also served as the foundation for the Reading First component of NCLBA.

While it is fairly obvious that years of reliable research went into identifying third grade as the "do or die" date by which students should learn to read, there is another reason for the early intervention focus. That reason is quite simple to understand. Helping early elementary students who are behind a grade level in reading is much less difficult than helping older middle and high school students rise several grade levels in reading. In fact, that task is exceedingly difficult for even the most skilled literacy interventionist. Even then, some might state that the task is near impossible.

Yet in many urban center schools throughout the United States, classrooms are flooded with students who are well beyond third grade and haven't learned to read and/or have little interest in the ways in which literacy is used and taught within the confines of school. So with students this far behind the curve, legitimate hesitancy creeps in, and skeptics are prompted to question whether there's sufficient justification for continued infusions of federal funding and other scant resources when the results are so poor.

Here is another frustrating aspect of this dilemma. In most cases, there's nothing more than excuses offered to explain the systemic and longstanding lack of progress. Even worse, some of these same excuses have circulated for decades, as have the same old implausible solutions for fixing them.

"THERE'S A REASON FOR THIS TREND THAT'S OUTSIDE THE CONTROL OF THE SCHOOLS" . . . AND OTHER LIBERAL EXPLANATIONS FOR URBAN SCHOOL FAILURE

Earlier in this chapter, the persistent pattern of academic failure exhibited by the Detroit public school system (and documented in the earlier referenced Brookings Institution study) was cited as an example of a school system that is beyond quick fixes and easy solutions. Yet while the pattern of failure in the Detroit public schools wasn't surprising because it was so firmly established and longstanding, some of the plausible explanations floated to defend the time-honored breakdown were alarming because of their seeming perpetuity and the fact that so little had changed over the course of time.

Study author Brian A. Jacob described the possible reasons for failure as an amalgam of diverse variables. They included a steady decline in state and local school funding levels, an anomalous rate of decentralization that impeded the Michigan Department of Education (MDOE) in its ability to develop coordinated educational reforms, charter school deregulation as well as MDOE failure to hold charters accountable, and last, concentrations of economic and political instability in the state's urban areas that have stubbornly persisted over the decades (Lewis, 2015b).

In response to Jacob's point regarding the insufficiency of funding being explicitly linked to the historically low scores, Michigan State Representative Tim Kelly, then-chairman of the House Education Committee, completely rejected the argument that school funding inequities played any role whatsoever. According to Kelly, "Michigan is one of the highest spending states in terms of educating students . . . if you look at local, federal and state, it's about $10,000 or more per pupil. . . . There is a silly correlation saying just because you throw money at the problem, things will get better" (Lewis, 2015b).

One of the most striking features of Jacob's explanation, however, is the intransigence of school failure, as well as how reminiscent his rationalization is to past attempts purporting to help shed light on the abysmal school failure rates. For example, in his groundbreaking work titled *The Urban School: A Factory for Failure* (1973), nationally prominent education researcher Ray Rist conducted a three-year longitudinal study of three urban school classrooms at the Attucks Elementary School in St. Louis, Missouri. He followed an all-black class (with all-black teachers) from kindergarten through second grade.

Rist's research spanned from September 1967 to January 1970. It incorporated participant and nonparticipant observations of school, home, and peer experiences with a group of black students he had tracked since they were in kindergarten. His central research question focused on urban schools' ability to shape and determine the academic identities of those students who would, ultimately, be cast as academic winners and academic losers. Further, he sought to identify the ways in which teacher behavior nurtured and supported those student classifications.

At the study's conclusion, Rist determined that "the single most influential variable to which teachers responded was the social class background of the student," as race had been taken out of contention. Race wasn't a factor in this study because both the students and teachers included in it were African American (Rist, 1973, p. 242). Academic winners, as identified by their teachers, arrived at school each day ready to learn; they were neat and clean in appearance as well as came from traditional two-parent families that also happened to be middle class; and last, they had well learned the school's overt and covert curricula (Rist, 1973).

Conversely, students deemed unready to learn and identified as academic losers were oftentimes those considered unclean and who smelled of urine; they came from poor, single-parent homes; and had failed to grasp either the school's covert or overt curricula (Rist, 1973). Needless to say, the teachers' expectations for the students (one way or the other) became self-fulfilling prophecies. Thus, one of Rist's biggest takeaways was that schools reinforce and perpetuate existing societal inequalities despite the fact that they play no role in creating them. They merely exacerbate an already-present cultural divide.

So what would be the remedy in this case or the most effective school reform that could be explored under the circumstances described in the Rist study? In an honest and forthright manner, Rist stated the following: "There are no universal antidotes one can offer to insure that all schools will become humane and rewarding places in which teachers and students can spend time together" (Rist, 1973, p. 255). Without a doubt, it seems even more challenging for urban schools serving minority populations to become such places.

Twenty-five years later, researcher Jean Anyon described thoroughly dreadful urban center classrooms in the context of a study she completed in Newark, New Jersey, prior to her early death. Anyon's study included first-hand accounts of hearing a teacher tell a young girl that her breath "smelled like dog shit" (Anyon, 1997, p. 29) or other teachers making comments to their students such as "You're disgusting; you remind me of children I would see in a jail" (p. 29) and "If I had a gun I'd kill you. You're all hoodlums" (p. 30).

By far, however, the most disturbing comment overheard was directed at a young African American fourth-grader whose mother happened to work as a prostitute. Her teacher told her, "Your mother's pussy smells like fish. That's what stinks around here" (Anyon, 1997, p. 29). Also note that the male teacher who made this comment had no prior education courses or teacher preparation, had been identified in catastrophic terms by school staff, and had volumes of parental complaints lodged against him. Yet, he was ultimately awarded tenure on the strength of his outside political connections in the City of Newark (Anyon, 1997).

Now, while the comments overheard are undoubtedly salacious and shocking, they pale in comparison to the teacher assaults on students that Anyon also witnessed.

> On eight occasions when I was working with teachers in their classrooms, I saw . . . teachers, none of whom was considered to be an unusually harsh disciplinarian, smack a student with some force on the head, chest, or arm as if it were a routine occurrence. On numerous occasions I saw teachers grab students by the arm and shake them. No one reacted to these actions. (Anyon, 1997, p. 29)

The abuse these students suffered wasn't solely at the hands of their teachers. Anyon identified local residents employed by the school as stealing the children's food. "On five occasions that came to my attention during my work at the school, custodians or cafeteria workers stole, or left doors open for others to come in and steal, the food for the children's hot lunch. . . . During the few days following each theft, there was no lunch for the 497 free lunch students" (Anyon, 1997, p. 161).

Now, at the time during which Anyon's research was conducted, it was deemed highly controversial because the research methodology she used included the practice of deception. She told the unwitting research participants that she was studying and conducting professional development when in fact she was studying urban school reform and documenting what she saw and heard.

While many in the field of education (including the author) believe that Anyon's study serves as an incredibly rich contribution to the field, there are others who contend that the ends simply don't justify the means. This group firmly holds to the position that Anyon's work damaged the reputation of the Newark public school system, exploited and eroded trust, and made it much more difficult for subsequent researchers to gain access to any struggling New Jersey schools (especially those most in need of help).

It should be noted, however, that while many have challenged the methods used, there has been very little challenge to the veracity of Anyon's accounts of what she witnessed and heard in the respective schools and classrooms she observed.

Yet despite all that she witnessed and heard, Anyon naively casts urban school reform as a possibility under the right circumstances in the end. Although she did acknowledge that there was a long history of inferior quality that could be ascribed to Newark's public school system and she was able to trace the downward spiral to about the mid-1930s, she remained guardedly optimistic about the plausibility of school reform in places like Newark (Anyon, 1997).

Frankly, Anyon's insistence that reform remained within the realm of possibility seems more akin to a pipe dream than the harsh reality that many have come to accept. We've simply run out of options here. Thus, the time is now that we must ask hard questions and accept the unblinking truth. To those who routinely defend urban schools, the following questions should be posed: *Isn't two hundred years enough time to make a determination that they have failed? Would you send your children to this school system that you're defending? What solutions are you proffering?*

Further, there's never anything new or different offered when it comes to explaining the longstanding record of chronic and pervasive failure maintained by too many of the nation's urban public schools. For these reasons as well as others, there has been widespread debate, discussion, and movement to shutter perpetually failing urban schools that disserve the communities forced to rely upon them and afford those communities access to viable educational options that have been consistently linked with academic success.

SO WHAT'S THE CONCLUSION?

True reform will occur only if we start to think about urban school reform in a very different way and revisit solutions that the public might not have previously been ready to entertain. Thus, it is critical that educational alternatives be proffered and those options can and should include school choice and vouchers, as well as charter schools and competent homeschooling.

Therefore, all educational alternatives should be offered, and those options should include charter schools, vouchers, and school choice, as well as changes to the school funding formulas that fund most states' K–12 public school systems.

Chapter Five

Can Competition Serve as the Jump Start That Failing Urban Public Schools Need to Get Their Acts Together?

> Basic Prerequisite of market choice: people have the freedom to switch from one alternative to another when they think it would be beneficial to do so. (Chubb and Moe, 1990, p. 32)

At this point in your reading, it is hoped that there has been sufficient evidence presented to convince you of one primary point. Here it is: The nation's urban public schools are deeply troubled. That turmoil is, effectively, the culmination in a chain of systemic and pervasive problems that have historically plagued them.

Rather than abating over time, those problems have intensified and continue to rage on with no end in sight unless decisive and sweeping reform is undertaken. Contrary to popular belief, that reform doesn't occur from within the system of government schooling. Time's up on the belief that any legitimate reform effort situated within most urban public schools can be even remotely successful. Enough time has elapsed to yield fruit, but no such fruit has manifested. So now, it will be an external force that disturbs the status quo, catalyzes change, and makes anew from the wreckage.

Despite the fact that liberal activists and defenders of urban public schools have consistently tried to convince the American public otherwise, pointing out these legion problems isn't manufactured, hyperbolic, or the result of an organized campaign solely designed to distort the facts for the purpose of making urban schools look bad. The real facts and figures belie this mythology; instead, a truth that many of us have known for quite some time has surfaced.

Surprisingly, even liberal defenders of urban public schools (like Pedro Noguera) are compelled to acknowledge the insidious and stubborn nature of the problems afflicting urban center schools. In his 2003 *City Schools and the American Dream: Reclaiming the Promise of Public Education*, Noguera admits that there's little proof that urban center schools well educate the students who attend them. But, quixotically, he still concludes that even the inferior urban public schools are better than nothing at all.

> The bottom line is that even when there is little evidence of educational efficacy, urban public schools still provide services that are desperately needed by poor families, and federal and state policies offer few alternatives. In the absence of genuine alternatives, even failing public schools retain a dependent although disgruntled constituency base because they are typically the only social institution that provides a consistent source of stability and support to impoverished families. (Noguera, 2003, p. 6)

Huh? So because the families are impoverished, they should accept substandard schooling and the subpar social services provided by these schools? Why? Because substandard schooling/services are better than no schooling/services at all? Hmmm. . . . Pass the Tylenol please!

There is any number of people who would take Noguera to task for these statements. There is an even larger contingent that would contend that the statements are condescending, pejorative, and belittling. There are still others who refuse to accept that simply because the bulk of families utilizing urban center schools are poor doesn't mean that they should also be willing to gratefully accept society's castoffs and tolerate what affluent parents haven't and wouldn't. Being poor is neither synonymous with being less deserving nor accepting (out of necessity) what is wholly unacceptable.

There's an unwavering fact that has been presented throughout this text: The vast majority of urban center schools throughout this nation are failures and, contrary to Noguera's point, beyond redemption. The lion's share of these schools produces graduates who are unable to decode texts, comprehend texts with a reading level as low as fourth grade or above sixth through eighth grade, and for far too many, higher-order thinking is undeniably out of the range of possibility.

LONGITUDINAL OUTCOMES OF URBAN PUBLIC SCHOOLING

In a stunning turn of events during June 2018, Federal District Court Judge Stephen Murphy III declared that there was no legitimacy to a class-action suit filed on behalf of students in Detroit's worst-performing public schools. The suit alleged that Detroit public school students had been denied their constitutional right of "access to literacy." The plaintiffs contended that the gross levels of Detroit public school underfunding, mismanagement, and discrimination had "woefully underprepared them for life after high school" (Fortin, 2018).

For verification of the students' claims, the reader is referenced back to *Unlearning Failure's* chapter 4. It should also be noted that the state of Detroit public schools litigated by the plaintiffs came after the school district had been declared insolvent or bankrupt and Governor Rick Snyder had approved a $617-million bailout and debt restructuring plan.

This case, in particular, garnered a great deal of interest primarily because of the perceived inexplicability of the judge's ruling and the cognitive dissonance it engendered for most of those reading the decision. Yet it wasn't the first such lawsuit to identify "access to literacy" as a constitutional right. A lawsuit filed during December 2017 on behalf of students at three Los Angeles schools (including La Salle Avenue Elementary School, Van Buren Elementary School, and Promise Preparatory Academy) was actually the first to float said claim.

In fact, that suit was the first in the entire United States to seek recognition of a citizen's constitutional right to literacy according to the plaintiffs' lawyers (Hauser, 2017). While many remain fairly optimistic about the odds of winning this particular litigation, caution is still warranted as it proceeds. The optimism is based, in part, on the belief that cases like this one appear to fare better in state courts rather than those at the US district level.

Rutgers Professor Emeritus Paul Trachtenberg, whose work is often cited with respect to issues regarding the nexus of constitutional law and education, stated that "lawsuits like this one are typically filed—and have a better chance of success—in state-level courts. In theory, it would be a great breakthrough to have the federal courts recognize education as a fundamental right. . . . But I see no chance of that happening in my lifetime" (Fortin, 2018).

Herein lies the most disheartening aspect of these lawsuits: the students parked in these failing schools and their advocates recognize something essential and key that many courts appear unwilling to even acknowledge. Without adequate access to quality educational and literacy opportunities, the fate of these young people is basically sealed. Without such quality experiences, they are regrettably destined to fall short of their collective promise as well as the potential to lead successful, productive lives.

For example, the results of the Educational Testing Service's Programme for the International Assessment of Adult Competencies (PIAAC) Survey offered depressing news on the literacy skills of US adults (Sabatini, 2015). Designed to test the literacy skills of US adults against those of adults in five other countries, the survey sample included the four English-speaking nations of the United States, Canada, the United Kingdom, and Ireland, as well as two where English isn't the dominant language, Italy and Spain (Sabatini, 2015). There were four score categories encompassing Below Level I, At Level I, Level II, and Level III.

The PIAAC Survey's most compelling finding was that the US Below Level I and At Level I groups scored below every other English-speaking country that had been included in the sample, as well as those groups from the non-English-speaking countries (Italy and Spain) that were also part of the study (Sabatini, 2015). Now, there is no contention here that all of the adults surveyed attended urban public schools. But there is a suggestion that a large percentage of them did.

The following statistics seem to verify that many of the same demographics impacted by failing urban schools appear to be those demographics that are also identified as being illiterate or academically underprepared. For instance, approximately 20 percent of those who graduated from high school with diplomas weren't capable of reading those diplomas, and 21 percent of girls with literacy challenges became pregnant before they were financially and emotionally prepared to do so, as compared to 5 percent of girls who were declared proficient readers (Lake, 2016). Additionally, 75 percent of US welfare recipients weren't considered proficient readers in 2016 (Lake, 2016).

Regarding worker productivity, the proportion of US workers categorized as illiterate cost the nation approximately $225 billion per year (Lake, 2016). Further, while some have asserted that there is a nexus between low literacy levels and low wage earning, the true link is between low literacy levels and unemployment (ProLiteracy America, 2003).

A survey conducted on behalf of the American Management Association's member and client companies concluded that, for firms testing for below high school graduate-level skill, 34.1 percent of job applicants lacked the requisite literacy skills and approximately 90 percent of those applicants weren't hired (ProLiteracy America, 2003).

Please note (at this point) that a conscious authorial decision has been made within the context of this discussion to focus on the longitudinal impact that urban public schools have on students' economic preparedness and earning potential. Here is another attendant point highlighted in this transactional conversation with the reader: there isn't the mere focus on urban center students' eventual suitability to become workers.

Unlearning Failure has a bigger vision for these students and, as such, wants to explore whether they've been adequately prepared to assume roles like business owner and entrepreneur. Although expected, it is no less sad that urban public schools would be deemed even bigger failures if they were evaluated on the basis of whether they actually prepared students for more than following orders and development into compliant workers for low-wage-earning jobs that have and will continue to be automated into the foreseeable future.

As a result of the inferior education the vast majority of these students have received, most will never be able to envision themselves as or become anything other than a new generation of adults who have failed to earn enough money to elevate themselves out of poverty or even dare to dream about home or business ownership that so many other young people and demographics have captured because society and their schools well equipped them with the proper tools to do so.

For instance, although there is good news about the rate of US black business ownership with its steady increases over the past fifteen years, people of African descent continued to substantially lag behind other racial groups in respect to business ownership during 2016. While blacks constitute approximately 12 percent of the adult population in the United States, they were owners of a mere 3.3 percent of businesses younger than two years old (Simon and Overberg, 2016). Contrastingly, white-owned firms comprised 81 percent of businesses during the same time frame, while 9.7 percent were Asian owned and 5.8 percent were owned by Latinos (Simon and Overberg, 2016).

Overall, black-owned businesses trended smaller and less profitable as well. The sales mean at black-owned firms was approximately $915,000, while white-owned businesses recorded an average of $2.38 million. Asian-owned businesses brought in $1.19 million, and profits for Latino-owned businesses came in at $1.12 million (Simon and Overberg, 2016).

There have been many explanations proffered to contextualize these patterns related to the stagnant growth of black-owned businesses, including the fact that people of African descent often start out in life with fewer monetary assets and were harder hit by the Great Recession of 2007–2009. In fact, many haven't fully recovered more than eight years later. It has also been suggested that black-owned businesses are heavily reliant upon the public sector. That dependency leaves them at risk when there are declines in governmental spending and affirmative action policies are either weakened or unenforced.

Yet there is another plausible explanation as well. Business ownership/entrepreneurship isn't presented as a consistent and reliable option to children of African descent in the schools they attend, especially those schools that are failing and based in urban centers. For our purposes, *entrepreneurship* "is 'the pursuit of an opportunity irrespective of existing resources' and 'entrepreneurs' [are] those who perceive themselves as pursuing such opportunities" (Krueger and Brazeal, 1994, p. 91).

Therefore, there is a crisis for black children in the following respect. Too many fail to envision themselves as pursuing entrepreneurial prospects because the clear majority hasn't been exposed to role models who own their respective businesses. Further, schools (and urban ones, in particular) are doing an inadequate job of exposing all students to the tools and dispositions needed to make entrepreneurship a viable career option.

For example, a prior seminal study conducted by Walstad and Kourilsky (1998) found that of the 842 respondents surveyed and for whom complete data were available, three-fourths of high school–aged students identifying as black expressed the desire to own their own businesses. Thus, they were significantly more predisposed to own than their white counterparts. Yet the majority (53 percent) of black respondents wasn't acquainted with anyone (including parents) who actually owned a business. In contrast, less than 38 percent of white students were unfamiliar with anyone owning a business.

Now we arrive at another authorial decision made regarding *Unlearning Failure* and its discussion of illiteracy and academic underpreparedness. While there is an abundance of data that link illiteracy and academic underpreparedness to crime or some level of involvement with the criminal justice system, that connection will not be broached comprehensively here. The decision is predicated on the following.

In too many instances, the statistics are deceptive. Frequently, the data fail to account for racial bias, sentencing disparities, and/or the appropriate teasing apart of low-level drug offenses from violent crime. Additionally, these omissions give the statistics an exaggerated degree of importance, bolster prevailing racial stereotypes, and lead to much less finely nuanced conclusions or findings than we should anticipate or accept.

Further, some would contend that the ways that urban center schools (themselves) are managed and the harsh disciplinary methods they have traditionally imposed on black and Hispanic students contribute to the proportion of those students who then face imprisonment or criminal justice system involvement. The reality is that too great a number of urban public schools resemble prisons and simulate the feeling of being imprisoned for the students who attend them. In addition, the school discipline imposed disproportionately impacts black students, male and female.

In many urban "government" schools, security measures such as metal detectors at points of ingress and egress, random (albeit regularly scheduled) metal detector checks of students' persons, drug testing, random sweeps for contraband, security cameras, armed police or security guards posted at school checkpoints, and the use of canine officers are commonplace (Finn and Servoss, 2015). Further, despite the prison-like atmosphere replicated in most of these schools, it is notable that the vast majority of well-publicized school shootings do not occur inside of them.

Additionally, black students are approximately 2.3 times more likely to be suspended than white students (Toldson, McGee, and Lemmons, 2015). "Students across the United States who are suspended from school are less likely ... to obtain a high school diploma and ... bachelor's degree ... and are more likely to be arrested, arrested multiple times, and sentenced to confinement in a correctional facility" (Shollenberger, 2015, p. 41). So back to the point we started with, urban center public schools must assume their fair share of responsibility for feeding the school-to-prison pipeline.

Last on this point, it should be relatively clear that there are multiple other ways in which these students' lives and, by extension, society are impacted by urban public schools' incapacity to adequately prepare the students who attend them. Yet most rush to emphasize the link between that failure and crime in a manner that hints at racialized bias in a none-too-subtle fashion. We all know, however, that the majority of ways in which urban schools fail extends far beyond students getting caught up in the criminal justice system.

Tame, turnaround measures and gradual reforms have proven ineffective in fixing urban public schools. So we must now be willing to consider out-of-the-box alternatives and a dramatic overhaul of these failure factories. Such bold and decisive acts would help us fulfill our societal obligation to the large numbers of urban students stuck in place and languishing within them. Thus far, there has been neither punishment nor incentive for urban schools to afford students a better quality of education because there have been relatively few consequences for failing to do so.

COULD COMPETITION JUMP START A RENAISSANCE IN URBAN PUBLIC SCHOOLING?

Often the ardent support for US public education, even what is presently failing and has failed for an exceedingly long period of time, is grounded in the philosophy of Socialism. A Socialist economic system is predicated upon the belief that all means of making money and acquiring wealth are controlled by the people rather than the government, in addition to the conviction that the management and sharing of the economy must be used to advance the collective good. It would also be fair to state that the US-based movement of Socialism experienced a resurgence with Bernie Sanders's 2016 presidential campaign.

Many of the most vocal advocates for maintaining failed public schools in urban centers are also proponents of socialized health care and the institution of a millionaires' tax that they claim would quixotically motivate millionaires to pay their fair share, in addition to being among the loudest and most strident voices decrying wealth inequality.

It is difficult to follow the train of thought here regarding the millionaires' tax, in particular. As many millionaires are also job creators, innovators, and employers of large numbers of people, in which ways aren't they fulfilling their duty to pay their fair share? Thus, this demand falls of its own weight because it doesn't serve the public good and too closely resembles the incitement of class warfare.

Other wacky Socialist proposals floated for the putative purpose of preserving the collective good include concepts like *free college for all* and *universal income*. As free college for all circulated during the Sanders presidential campaign, most Americans have heard of it. Yet universal income is the new kid on the block. Through the use of fairly benign and innocuous language, it is defined as a "simple idea that would entail giving people enough money to meet their basic needs, providing everyone with an income floor" (Universal Income Project, 2016).

When presented in these magnanimous terms, who could possibly object to such a grand and noble cause? Well, for starters, those of us taxpayers for whom the concept has been translated in the following manner. Universal income would be yet another entitlement program whereby the federal government would use additional taxpayer funding to provide poor citizens with a baseline income regardless of whether they work or not.

For real?? It gets worse because Socialists seem to rarely think about the logistics of their half-baked plans or how such plans can be actualized in ways that fairly and equitably distribute this added financial burden across an already overtaxed populace. Rarely are proponents of universal income even able to answer the most basic questions regarding how the plan would work.

For example, despite possessing a snazzier and more sophisticated name, how does universal income differ from Aid to Families with Dependent Children (AFDC), established under the Social Security Act and first instituted in 1935? How is it different from Social Security itself and/or other federally sanctioned, antipoverty programs? Under the auspices of universal income, who would qualify for this new pot of money and how? Is everyone who presents a need entitled to funding or just the neediest? How do you distinguish between the needs of the two categories?

Last, there has been much discussion surrounding the fact that Social Security is virtually depleted. Some forecasts suggest that the system is already overdrawn. Others have predicted that it could become insolvent as soon as 2033. Aside from being unable to answer the tough questions set forth in the previous paragraph, many Socialists also seem clueless about the magnitude of the burden that they are calling upon other taxpayers to assume. That burden is made even heavier when one considers that these taxpayers are being asked to fund other people's priorities with their money but without their full consent.

Although they balk at the criticism that they are driven by a sense of entitlement that subordinates the moral compasses of those who disagree with them and instead privileges their own habitually distorted viewpoints, the truth belies the pushback and feigned indignation. The following statement from Leftist scholar Robin D. G. Kelley perfectly encapsulates the

Socialist mind-set that supports the continued existence of so many unsuccessful institutions, including urban public schools, and rarely calls upon them to improve or show evidence of success.

According to Kelley and in seamless alignment with the tenets of Socialism, he declares:

> Creating good jobs, rebuilding homes, improving the health of communities—in short, reversing a couple of centuries of deleterious social policy—costs a lot of money. We can afford it, if our country is willing to divert funds from war (foreign and domestic), substantially reduce the work week without cutting wages, and start forcing rich people and corporations to pay their fair share of taxes. Whether we ever create a state that puts working people's needs before corporations will depend on which vision of society we embrace. A well-paying, fulfilling job and a strong "safety net" in troubled times should be a basic right, not a handout or an entitlement. (1997, pp. 100–101)

Yet here is a glaring hole in Kelley's argument. On what authority does *he* determine what other US citizens should do with the tax money they are required to pay (by law)? Doesn't their tax money already go to funding national priorities and benefitting society's least of these? Despite the fact that he rejects the casting of his vision for a socially just society as an "entitlement," when anyone proposes wealth redistribution and payment for past societal wrongs, there's no other applicable word except . . . yes, entitlement. No, wait . . . there is another term, and it is called "cultural arrogance."

It is this cultural arrogance and desire to forcefully impose one's own beliefs onto others that led, in large measure, to the ascendancy of President Donald J. Trump. Now, for many of us centrists, Kelley's thoughts are quite far afield. In fact, they are so much so that a number of us can't even wrap our minds around or attempt to make logical sense of them. Yet Kelley's thoughts are made to appear insipid when juxtaposed against those of new Democratic rising star Adriana Ocasio-Cortez who, in a stunning upset, defeated longstanding congressman Joe Crowley of New York's Fourteenth District during the June 2018 primary.

According to Ms. Ocasio-Cortez, the vast majority of the United States's contemporary economic problems can be attributed to a type of "no-holds-barred Wild West hyper-capitalism, what that means is profit at any cost. Capitalism has not always existed in the world, and it will not always exist in the world. When this country started, we did not operate on a capitalist economy."

Wow!! Again, where's the Tylenol? Contrary to the beliefs of Kelley and Ocasio-Cortez, however, it is Socialism for which the death knell rings. While there is absolutely no one contending that capitalism is the most equitable or dependable system, it is the only one that has stood the test of time. If we sought to compare the two, there is no doubt that capitalism is the hands-down winner.

It matters little whether one uses the former Soviet Union, the Eastern European bloc nations, or (most recently) Venezuela as examples to better illustrate the point. The fact remains that all three examples provide compelling evidence that "capitalism organizes the material affairs of humankind more substantially than socialism: that however inequitably or irresponsibly the marketplace may distribute goods, it does so better than the queues of planned economy" (Heilbroner, 1989, p. 98).

Market-driven competition or capitalism between sellers and buyers certifies that the profits earned by businesspeople and the prices paid by customers will often be driven down to the lowest point that a producer can accept while still maintaining enough money to produce the product (Walberg and Bast, 2003). "Competition and choice ensure that better goods and services are available at lower cost to consumers who most value them" (Walberg and Bast, 2003, p. 90).

Now, just because Socialists are misguided and apparently believe in a flawed and illogical economic premise doesn't mean that they aren't as well intentioned as those of us who are centrists, nor does it mean that they love our country any less. That isn't the author's premise. Yet it also isn't the central point of this discussion either. It is sheer lunacy to believe that one has the right to indefinitely spend other people's money on inferior products that are incredibly costly and simply do not work. Nowhere is this lunacy more obvious than when it comes to the nation's urban center public schools.

It wasn't until the early decades of the 1900s that we had anything resembling what we now know as public education in the United States. Prior to that time, schooling was a parochial matter controlled by local interests (Chubb and Moe, 1990). From the inception of government schooling in the United States, however, public schools have been exempted from the type of competition that every other American industry has been subject to. That lack of competition has been particularly detrimental to those students who have been compelled to attend these public schools, as *Unlearning Failure* has solidly established thus far.

The logic that applies to almost every other American industry seemingly doesn't apply to the nation's schools. In what universe does a business fail year after year, lose customers, and continue to produce inferior products, yet its doors remain open and it stays in business? For those of you who might find the statement regarding the loss of clientele/customers odd, you might wish to think of public school students as the schools' customers. When those students leave school prematurely or drop out of school altogether, they are also representative of lost customers or clients.

Current statistics suggest that more than 1.2 million US students drop out of high school each year. Deduced further, that's approximately one student every twenty-six seconds—or seven thousand per day (DoSomething.org, 2018). Regarding urban center public schools specifically, many of them would be included among the two thousand schools presently designated as "dropout factories" (DoSomething.org, 2018).

"Dropout factories" are labeled as such because they fail to graduate approximately 60 percent of the students attending them. Furthermore, the term also acknowledges their active participation in maintaining the stubbornly persistent 50 percent rate of students leaving school prematurely (DoSomething.org, 2018).

In the real world, businesses simply don't operate this way, nor should they. For far too long and in the most unpretentious of terms, public or government schooling has been one of the only American businesses for which traditional industry rules haven't appeared to apply. For that reason, *Unlearning Failure* is making the case that said exemption should quickly come to an end.

Market-driven competition or capitalism is a core American value. It was actually written into the Declaration of Independence, originally penned in 1776, and the Articles of Confederation written the following year in 1777. Thus, contrary to Ms. Ocasio-Cortez's understanding, capitalism was prominently featured within the United States's earliest founding documents. Additionally, it distinguished us and provided us with our own distinctive identity as we divorced ourselves from British rule by forming the original thirteen colonies. Capitalism, by some accounts, served as a bulwark of American exceptionalism.

The inability to freely trade is listed as one among a plethora of reasons that motivated the colonists to initially seek independence from Britain. According to the Declaration, King George III had erred by "cutting off our Trade with all Parts of the World." Next, the Articles of Confederation set forth the following guarantee that each member of the Confederation "agrees to defend each other in the event of attacks made against any of them because of religion independence, trade, or any other reason." Please note that "trade" is specifically referenced.

Further, many of the services that (over time) we—as a society—have grown accustomed to receiving from government-run providers—including the servicing of sewers and drinking water, roads, parks, zoning, traffic lights, mass transit, and yes, schools—were originally delivered through private firms, civic organizations, and/or individuals (Walberg and Bast, 2003). "Disappointment with the quality of government-run services in the United States and around the world led to efforts to return the production of a wide variety of commodities to the private sector" (Walberg and Bast, 2003, p. 230).

There may be no government-run service that has evoked more disappointment and angst than urban public schools. As these schools have been considered the only game in town for many parents and caregivers of urban center students, they have felt no compulsion or urgency to compete for either students or resources. They also haven't experienced the repercussions of having to close their school's doors because they have consistently produced an inferior product.

TIME'S UP... SCHOOL CHOICE NOW!

In a competitive marketplace in which some schools will likely thrive while others fail and board up their doors, a higher quality of education will likely be afforded to urban school youngsters who have waited for longer periods of time than they deserve to or should have. *Unlearning Failure* makes the case that, when urban center schools operate in the same way that other competitive industries do and start to feel the discomfort associated with true and rigorous competition, we'll see a change in their performance and their outputs will be of an improved quality.

Various studies conducted on the effects of traditional school choice appear to suggest that public schools do, in fact, respond to competition by improving the quality of schooling they proffer and enhancing their focus on more stringent cost-containment strategies (Hoxby, 1998). Real challenges resulting from increased competition have been documented as producing consequential improvement in student test scores as well as their rates of educational attainment and wage-earning capacities (Hoxby, 1998).

Yet these public school responses are not solely dependent upon whether the targeted schools experience a loss of students or not. For some of them, the loss of students alone can be survivable. It is the loss, when exacerbated by the weight of fiscal rewards and penalties associated with gaining or losing students, that poses the far greater challenge and proves more difficult to navigate (Hoxby, 1998). When there's little financial incentive to hold onto students, the reaction to competition will likely be muted. Conversely, when the fiscal imperative is great, there will be a much more intense pushback from public schools.

When it is demanded of them that they convince parents and caregivers of their product's quality (in this instance, education) rather than gain precious cargo by default, we'll see a drastic change. When they are asked to confirm that they are capable of providing students with an excellent education that will prepare them to lead successful, adult lives, that's when we'll see change. Finally, when the change they are purporting to make can be qualitatively *and* quantifiably measured, that's when true reform will occur.

This book in no way espouses or advocates for the destruction of public education as we know it. There isn't even a desire to see the majority of urban public schools shuttered, because such an act would marginalize the efforts of urban school teachers, administrators, and staff who make a way out of no way daily during the 180-day school year. This cadre of dedicated educators has been moderately successful in educating the students in their charge, despite the many and varied obstacles they encounter each day. For their herculean efforts, they should be applauded instead of scorned.

It is clearly recognized that there are those who believe that the US Department of Education should cease to exist and public education should be totally privatized. For a number of those making such claims, their principal assertion is rooted within the US Constitution itself. They fervently contend that there is no Department of Education delineated within the pages of that founding document. Usually, such criticisms are also associated with Originalist and Textualist interpretations of that deeply cherished text, the Constitution.

Originalists embrace the US Constitution as fixed and knowable. Thus, its words and attributes are considered immutable and invariable over the course of time. The Textualist read of the Constitution is ever so slightly different. According to Textualist interpretation, the structure and text of the document (as understood by the average person at the time it was written) takes on arch significance and never changes.

While all are correct regarding their initial premise that the Department of Education fails to appear in the Constitution, even the most cursory of reads would have yielded that as an infrequently argued and indisputable point. Was there ever any claim made to the contrary? Instead, chances are that a much more reasonable and consequential assertion was put forth.

Here it goes. The US Constitution was originally set forth to provide us (the people) with broad and immutable principles by which to govern ourselves. The US Constitution commenced as a governance document laying out the powers and limitations of the United States's three coequal branches of government: legislative, executive, and judicial. From its inception, the US Constitution served as a guiding document outlining each branch's governance structure and function.

Therefore, it might never have been intended that all future government offices would be envisioned and memorialized in that document, as there would be no way of anticipating a need that far into the future. It is highly doubtful that our founders even gave minimal thought to the shape of education going forward, especially in consideration of the fact that "most schools in the United States were privately owned and managed but funded by government subsidies as well as tuition. This arrangement held sway from the founding of the first colonies until the middle of the nineteenth century" (Walberg and Bast, 2003, p. 57).

Now, it should furthermore be acknowledged that the cries for these types of dramatic reforms from groups other than those discussed in the preceding paragraphs are quite possibly the result of an understandable anger about and frustration with a system that has been so costly and flawed over the centuries without much to show for the effort. It is also fair to state that, in most instances, those hollering the loudest for such draconian courses of action aren't educators.

Let's establish up front that the argument proffered by these critics is grounded in a fallacious premise. Many of them have come from the corporate world and think that the same strategies employed to ensure business success can be effectively replicated and used to reform K–12 education. Not! The same skills required for success in industry or even parenting (for that matter) don't translate easily or well when we're discussing public education.

Here is yet another germane point particular to this discussion and serving as a refutation to the call for abolishment of public education. There will always be children for whom there's no other alternative except to attend their neighborhood schools. Those youngsters are just as entitled to a first-rate education as are those whose parents/caregivers have the ability to purchase or acquire such an education for them found outside the confines of their communities.

So for this group of students, privatized education will probably do little to improve their lots in life. There isn't even a guarantee that some privatized educational facilities would be willing to set up shop in these communities where success is uncertain and therefore profit is just as dubious. In the end, this group of students—in particular—will likely continue to languish without viable outside options; yet this time they'll do so without even the benefit of the safety net previously in place.

Still another counterpoint for these critics would include the following. Schools differ from other industries in the following respect. The raw product with which schools are charged with working is children. Furthermore, these children oftentimes can't advocate for themselves or effectively communicate their needs all the time. In some instances, their parents are unwilling to or incapable of the level of advocacy that schools can more easily deliver.

There are times when the parents' lack of capacity hangs on their acknowledged or unacknowledged personal failings. Yet there are far more times when the sheer number and force of the outside variables bearing down on them impede their ability to maximally function and narrowly restrict their foci to ensuring their own survival as well as that of their children.

Regardless of their home lives or the circumstances that they have been forced to endure, the children serve as the centerpiece for this collective effort and are most important here. They necessitate a special level of nurturance and care that extends beyond their cognitive development and includes an emphasis on emotional and social growth as well. Although admittedly imperfect, the educators in those children's lives fulfill that necessary and basic function for them, especially as many of those children have come to depend upon us to deliver that standard of care.

While there might be wide agreement among all on the point that schools should be held to a higher standard than they are presently, it is just as important to acknowledge that using business and medical models (hook, line, and sinker) for the purpose of evaluating the efficacy of public education or shaping its improvement has had and will continue to have disastrous consequences. In a similar fashion, comparative models that hold the United States's educational performance against a standard witnessed in other countries with widely disparate demographics, customs, and educational systems is just as woefully inept.

Yet none of the information presented in this section changes one very basic fact. Too many urban public schools continue to fail. It also doesn't change the fact that not all of the community's public schools are needed, especially in those instances in which they aren't properly functioning and have failed to do so for quite some time now. So *Unlearning Failure* simply puts forth a societal challenge.

SO WHAT'S THE CHALLENGE?

The book advances the thought that students in urban centers should no longer be hamstringed by their ZIP codes. It argues that those students be presented with the same educational options and choices that more affluent parents (in higher tax brackets) have afforded their children for quite some time now because they have the resources to do so. Just because many urban parents/caregivers don't have that same access to cash doesn't mean that their children should be forced to tolerate inferior schooling that has failed them for generations at this point in time.

Unlearning Failure is predicated upon the firm belief that, when the playing field is leveled and students (regardless of race, ethnicity, socioeconomic status, or religion) are offered equitable educational opportunities, many of them will succeed. We're not just discussing success that is relegated to the academic in nature. No, we think big here! So we're anticipating that with the right tools, these students (as well) will excel in life.

There is no redistribution ideology being proffered here either! So while the needs of poor students in urban centers are extremely pressing, there is a parallel desire (on the part of this author) to see the children of those parents/caregivers who can afford to purchase a higher quality of education continue to academically soar and personally thrive. Yet they should be able to do so in a way that guarantees more money in their parents' pockets that can be used to support and sustain their own efforts to educate their own children.

When discussing this group of parents in particular, there has seemingly been very little concern for the injustice that has been traditionally meted out to them. It almost appears impolitic to mention it, in fact. Yet fairness must be distributed to all if it is to be credible. Therefore, we must do something to right this wrong that is disproportionately impacting those parents who can afford to exercise school choice.

After all, it is this group of parents that is legally required to contemporaneously pay for the educational choices they make for their own children while also subsidizing their local public school systems with their respective tax dollars, despite the fact that those schools may not be of any true value to them. There must be educational options and school choice for all rather than for some. Not only is that the American way, it is also what is considered fair and just in a civil society.

Chapter Six

What Is School Choice?

*Why Is It the Only Viable Alternative to
Failing Urban Schools in the New Millennium?*

> Because education involves teaching children about right and wrong, about what is important in life, it must be controlled by individual families, not by politicians and bureaucrats. No monopoly system can adequately reflect the values of all parents in a diverse society. (Boaz, 1997, p. 242)

WHAT ARE THE TWO TRADITIONAL FORMS THAT US SCHOOL CHOICE HAS TAKEN?

Oftentimes when the topic of "school choice" is raised, the general public views it in a decontextualized manner and seemingly reacts as if the concept is a new and unfamiliar one, a contemporary phenomenon of sorts. That belief in the "newness" of the concept is an erroneous one, however. School choice is "such an established feature of American education that it is almost taken for granted" (Hoxby, 1998, p. 47).

For some sectors of the US parent/caregiver population, school choice is neither new nor inherently different from what they have done since the country's inception. In fact, it is a practice upon which parents/caregivers (with more financial resources and privilege) have traditionally relied and of which they—on behalf of their children—continue to avail themselves.

School choice has been historically defined as the ability to choose where one's children attend school, and it has taken on two distinctive forms. From the start of American schooling, school choice has almost exclusively been viewed as a decision between attendance in a fiscally autonomous public school district and/or in a private school.

CHOOSING FISCALLY AUTONOMOUS SCHOOL DISTRICTS

For those choosing among public school districts, the decision has often been predicated upon where that family chooses to live. In a number of communities throughout the United States, a community's ample property tax base bolsters its capacity to transform its neighborhood public schools into ones that rival the lion's share of private schools.

Public education for a given community is a cost customarily assumed by the state and its local municipalities. As per the respective state, there will be an adjustable percentage of the state's annual budget (in the form of direct school aid) that is distributed to its local school districts. Local governments are then held responsible for covering the difference between the aid awarded through the state, federal funding sources, and the actual cost of the public school–related expenditure being made.

Aside from state and federal funding, municipalities are almost totally reliant upon property taxes and discretionary user fees as mechanisms for generating sufficient revenue to pay for those local services that residents believe they need and/or to which they feel entitled (New Jersey League of Municipalities, 2017). Chief among these services is education for their children.

So when it comes to school choice, here's how it has traditionally operated for large numbers of parents/caregivers who have chosen to utilize their local public schools: the more affluent the community in which a particular family resides or to which they have decided to move, the greater the likelihood that its neighborhood school system will be of a superior quality.

In those instances in which there is a scarcity of quality schooling in a particular community, many within the aforementioned group (with the means to) will simply relocate in an effort to secure the highest quality educational resources for their children. It is a nonstarter that parents with larger amounts of discretionary cash and higher incomes at their disposal have the ability to self-select into communities with excellent school systems. With this knowledge in hand, most realtors use local school systems as bargaining chips when it comes to sealing homeownership deals.

School choice has historically been less of an issue for parents residing in affluent suburbs than it has for those living in urban, predominantly low-income neighborhoods. Over the course of time, suburban parents have consistently exercised de facto school choice. They have applied this power by deciding to live in those communities that match their desires for their children as well as suit their needs regarding the quality of local public schools.

Further, they have weighed and carefully considered the dollar amount of property taxes that they can both reasonably afford and will be necessitated in order to sustain and enhance those public schools. Last on this specific point, they have contemplated whether those local school districts will provide an ample array of extracurricular offerings designed to address their children's social and emotional needs in a competent manner as well.

In US Census data gathered during the month of October 2015 that identified the social and economic characteristics of students enrolled throughout US schools, it was determined that with a total of 9.6 million families with children in grades K–12 that also disclosed annual incomes of $75,000 or more (the highest income bracket measured), 87 percent of that demographic had children who only attended public schools, while 11 percent had children who solely attended private ones (CAPE, 2018). There was a remaining 3 percent of children who went to both types of schools (CAPE, 2018).

Moreover, it stands to reason that the 87 percent of high-income families with children attending public schools (referenced in the Census study) would be the same group distinguished throughout this section as residing in or moving to communities with affordably excellent school systems. After all, why would there be a need for attendance at a private school with tuitions ranging from $10,740 to $25,180 (CAPE, 2018) when the public schools in one's community are of equivalent worth and their respective costs are already included in one's property taxes?

If taken at face value and without the consideration of potentially broader implications, the decision made by these financially better-off families is a reasonable one that could be commonly appreciated by most. After all, nearly everyone understands the necessity of protecting one's self-interests and providing one's children with the best possible start in life. Yet there's so much more packed within this decision than surfaces upon initial glance.

While the type of choice exercised by families with the means to move their children to better public school districts is easily comprehended, it is concurrently problematic with far-reaching societal impact. First, although it is a clear and indisputable benefit to the aforementioned families, it would also be accurate to state that these relocations further buttress longstanding patterns of firmly ensconced residential segregation. At this point in your reading, you know well that residential segregation has almost single-handedly reversed any school desegregation gains made post–*Brown v. Board of Education of Topeka*.

Second, while one would be hard pressed to find anyone who would begrudge another parent's desire to do what is best for her/his children, it is just as important to remember that there is a flip side to that coin. That opposite side of the coin is crammed full of families that do not have the generous cash reserves required to fund moves to more affluent neighborhoods, despite any feelings of dissatisfaction they might harbor regarding their own local schools.

This group of families has been left with relatively few options, aside from remaining in low socioeconomic status (SES) neighborhoods and sending their children to public schools that they undoubtedly know are of inferior quality and, in some instances, outright failing. The only other viable alternative would be to take the financial hit associated with sending their children to private schools that they can little afford.

While there might be a fair number of critics who would suggest that this issue of inequality in schooling is of a much smaller scale than purported, the actual statistics confirm the broad scope of the dilemma. The fact remains that the real and serious problem of students being trapped in flailing and failing urban public schools is every bit as prevalent as books like *Unlearning Failure* have purported them to be.

According to 2010 US Census Bureau statistics, 80.7 percent of the US population resided in urban centers at the time of that count. Thus, the nation's total urban population at that time was 249,253,271, which represented a growth rate of 12.1 percent from 2000 to 2010. That ratio outperformed the nation as a whole, which grew at a less impressive 9.7 percent (Berg, 2012). Further, although there were heavy concentrations of poverty in rural areas, most American poverty—at that particular time—was concentrated in US cities.

In 2011–2015 Census data that were composed of American Community Survey statistics collected during those years, urban poverty stood at 16 percent. That rate was approximately 3 percentage points higher than the rate in US rural areas. That rural poverty rate held at 13.3 percent (Soergel, 2016).

What does poverty look like for children and adolescents in the United States? In 2014, approximately 39 percent of African American children and adolescents and 33 percent of Hispanic children and adolescents lived in poverty (American Psychological Association, 2018). Additionally, there was a greater propensity for African American and Hispanic youngsters to attend schools characterized as high poverty. This rate was significantly higher than the rate of comparable school attendance documented for those students' Asian American and white counterparts (American Psychological Association, 2018).

So there's one immutable fact undergirding any discussion specific to school choice: "American parents are not equally able to exercise choice" (Hoxby, 1998, p. 47). Although high-SES parents have customarily employed more choice as a result of having more public school districts and private schools incorporated into their choice sets, low-SES parents have consistently been denied such options. That withholding has had little to do with the strength of their wishes for their children's successful futures and everything to do with their inability to pay for a better set of educational options for their children.

The other form of school choice to which large numbers of parents/caregivers (with financial means) have availed themselves is private school attendance for their children. In contemporary America, this choice has been made with full knowledge that parents/caregivers would be required to pay twice for the service of education for their children, even in the event that they chose against utilizing the educational services provided through their respective townships or municipalities. Specifically, they would be concurrently paying private school tuition while subsidizing their neighborhood public schools with their taxable income.

PRIVATE SCHOOL ATTENDANCE

From the earliest days of our then-fledgling nation, the vast majority of US schooling was provided via private schools that received small-scale governmental subsidies at that time. During the period spanning 1640 through 1840, large numbers of private schools were also owned and managed by individuals, religious groups, and churches (Walberg and Bast, 2003). In translation, they were privately owned and operated as opposed to being designated as government schools.

Further, it was customary for taxpayer funding (in the form of land grants and/or tax money) to be earmarked for use by private schools. Yet all except the most indigent families were required to pay tuition (Walberg and Bast, 2003). This arrangement surrounding government subsidies remained in force until approximately the middle of the nineteenth century, and the rationale for the practice was based upon the belief that private schools served the common good and fulfilled a public need (Walberg and Bast, 2003).

Although it was difficult for historians to reach consensus on the obtainable data regarding private schooling at the country's inception, there appeared to be widespread and tacit agreement on the following facts. In 1840 and with the preponderance of schools being designated private, "the northern states recorded the highest literacy rates in the world (over 90 percent), higher even than literacy rates today [and] competition worked, even in education" (Walberg and Bast, 2003, p. 57).

Post-1840, however, there was a rapid decline in government aid to private schools. Payments were substantially lowered and increasingly regulated to the point that they became near nonexistent, except in Vermont and Maine. It should be additionally noted that Vermont and Maine continue to make taxpayer funding available to private schools into the present day (Walberg and Bast, 2003).

With the drop in government aid to private schools came a coincidental rise in and expansion of government-owned and -operated schools (Walberg and Bast, 2003). By the end of the nineteenth century, government schools had been bestowed a near monopoly throughout the nation, and with that prize came the bulk of government funding that had previously kept the nation's private schools afloat (Walberg and Bast, 2003).

Another interesting point in this discussion regarding government funding cuts to private schools is the seeming motivation behind those reductions. Apparently, the same strong anti-Catholic sentiment that *Unlearning Failure* identified earlier in the book as being associated with the Second Wave of US immigration also played an influential role here in the decision to halt public funding that had once gone almost exclusively to private schools.

As a matter of fact, that antipathy toward Catholics—that greeted many Second Wave immigrants as they arrived on the shores of the United States and concomitantly served as a key distinction in the way they were treated by other immigrants who were already here—prompted most states in the nation (with the previously noted exceptions of Vermont and Maine) to amend their constitutions for the purposes of restricting or prohibiting the dissemination of government aid to private schools (Walberg and Bast, 2003).

Yet there is one remarkable trait of private schooling in the United States: its enduring nature. Despite deleterious funding cutbacks and prohibitions on government aid, American private schools have stood the test of time. In contemporary eras during the twentieth century, private school enrollment hovered around 15 percent or lower for American K–12 students. This percentage reached an apex of just under 15 percent in the early 1960s and hit its nadir at 10 percent in 1980. The number rebounded slightly to 12 percent during the late 1990s (Hoxby, 1998).

During that time as well, religious schools continued to dominate the private school market, with roughly 90 percent of students attending a school that was affiliated with a religious group, and those groups included both Christian and non-Christian religious faiths (Hoxby, 1998). The clear majority of private school students (65 percent) attended a school linked in some way to the Catholic Church, and they included parochial, diocesan, and private Catholic schools. A remaining 10 percent of those private school students surveyed attended schools that were nonsectarian in nature (Hoxby, 1998).

Surprisingly, recent statistics on private school attendance have remained steady for the most part. In the fall of 2015, about 5.8 million students were enrolled in private elementary and secondary schools, which represented 10.2 percent of K–12 students in the United States (IES/NCES, 2018c). Of that number, 36 percent of private school students were enrolled in Catholic schools with another 39 percent enrolled in other religiously affiliated schools. The remaining 24 percent were enrolled in nonsectarian schools (IES/NCES, 2018c).

Racially, white students comprised the most significant private school enrollment during the fall of 2015. Sixty-six percent attended Catholic schools, 73 percent of white students attended other religious schools, and 65 percent went to nonsectarian schools. Black students constituted the second-largest enrollment share at other religious schools (11 percent), while 16 percent of Hispanic students comprised the second-largest enrollment share at Catholic schools (IES/NCES, 2018c).

The largest percentage of Asian students attended nonsectarian schools (9 percent) and that rate surpassed their demographic's attendance at either Catholic and/or other religious educational institutions (5 percent each). Correspondingly, the 6 percent of students identifying as biracial was larger at nonsectarian schools than it was at Catholic (4 percent) and other religious schools (3 percent). Last on this point, 1 percent or fewer of Pacific Islander and American Indian/Alaska Native students were enrolled at Catholic, other religious, and nonsectarian schools (IES/NCES, 2018c).

While there is evidence of an uneven dropoff over time for all private schools (except non-Catholic religious schools, where there is growth), again private schools have demonstrated an amazing stability from 1980 to the present day. That steadiness has been maintained for the lion's share of schools designated as private, with the exception of the nation's Catholic schools, which experienced a 29-percent erosion that is both stark and dramatic.

Unfortunately, the reasons for the Catholic school dropoff are understandable. Post-1840, at the point when they could no longer rely upon government subsidies, most private schools were obligated to identify new revenue streams in an effort to make up for the shortfall they were then experiencing as well as to simply keep their school doors open. Thus, the religious schools became dependent on parishioner donations and/or endowment income.

For example, Catholic elementary schools underwrote 50 percent of their costs with donations from local households. Catholic dioceses helped to further subsidize those schools with members of their various religious orders who agreed to serve as teachers and school administrators at little to no cost. This cost-saving stopgap measure relieved the Church of the responsibility of hiring much more expensive salaried laypeople for those positions (Hoxby, 1998). Catholic secondary school tuitions weren't subsidized to the same extent, but they were handled in the same fashion when it came to school staffing (Hoxby, 1998).

Throughout time, this particular cost-saving strategy of using clergy as school personnel significantly waned, especially in consideration of the fact that fewer priests and nuns have entered the Catholic religious orders over the course of the past five years. Globally, the number of Catholic priests has declined by as little as 136 to an astounding 415,656 in 2015, the last year for which data were accessible (Associated Press, 2018).

Although affiliation with women's religious orders quickly accelerated during the first half of the twentieth century and peaked at 181,421 sisters in 1966, those rates have steadily declined since that time (Gibson, 2017). Current statistics show such rates of affiliation at below 50,000 and representing a 72.5 percent dropoff (Gibson, 2017). As a result, the Catholic schools' fiscal reality has been altered, and they are now forced to assume the almost total cost of hiring salaried laypeople to serve as teachers and administrators.

Attendant, complicating factors have been specific to the willingness of local churchgoers to make contributions and the relative frequency of those donations. In a recent Gallup poll that looked at Catholic Church attendance spanning from 2014 to 2017, it was revealed that approximately 34 percent of US Catholics attended Mass each week during those years (Saad, 2018).

This shift marks an 11-percentage-point difference from 2005 to 2008 when 45 percent of Catholics attended weekly Mass and a 31 percent drop from 1955 when weekly attendance was at 75 percent (Saad, 2018). In an interesting twist, it should be noted that the number of baptized Catholics rose globally during this time as well, from 1.27 billion to nearly 1.29 billion (Associated Press, 2018).

Tithes and offerings weren't previously problematic when weekly church attendance rates were strong and the Catholic Church had not yet been rocked by the sex abuse scandal that has shaken its very core. For many, that scandal might have played the single largest role in drying up donations.

During the years from 2000 to 2010, allegations against approximately three thousand Catholic priests that (in some instances) were more than fifty years old were brought to adjudication before the Holy See, the central governing body of the Catholic Church. Additional allegations regarding the sexual abuse of minors by bishops, priests, and nuns have continued into the present day. Some of the most recent have been revealed as late as the summer of 2018. Although there are those who would look skeptically at the relationship between the drying up of Church coffers and the abuse scandal, the link is an explicit one for many others.

While authors' self-disclosures are widely frowned upon by most academic publishers, I must take the risk of personally interjecting here. As a practicing and devout Catholic, this section has been especially difficult for me to write. It is both shameful and horrific. While there are some who would express the belief that the Church should keep its criticisms internal, I am of a different mind-set. It is important for those outside the Church to know that many of us do not condone the depravity that has occurred.

The victims need our acknowledgment of the terrible wrong that has been done to them. They also need to know that there is a large contingent of Catholics who want to see them get the justice they so rightfully deserve. If we choose against publicly condemning iniquitous actions, we risk the chance of the atrocities occurring again. In order for there to be healing of the Catholic Church that many of us continue to love despite its numerous imperfections, we must openly speak about the Church's sins, acknowledge wrongs, and explore ways to help restore our beloved Church to its former strength.

So at this juncture, there might be readers who are sincerely pondering the following question: "What does the sex abuse scandal have to do with the Catholic schools?" Well, if parishioners feel less confident about the Church, they will be disinclined to support the Church's charitable efforts, with its schools being one of them. Therefore, church donations dwindle and annual fund-raising appeals go unheeded. On a related note, these sex abuse revelations shook the faith of parents considering Catholic schools as an option for their children, and that reaction is easily comprehended, as a parent's primary duty is to protect his/her child.

As a result of the scandal, declines in attendance and donations, as well as lower enrollments, many dioceses throughout the United States have been forced to make gut-wrenching decisions to shutter large numbers of their schools. Unfortunately, too many of those closures occurred in geographic areas where the schools were needed most, despite the fact that the parishes might be among the poorest.

"Parochial schools, quite apart from their sectarian purpose, have provided an educational alternative for millions of young Americans: they often afford wholesome competition with the public schools; and in some States they relieve substantially the tax burden incident to the operation of public schools" (Walberg and Bast, 2003, p. 254).

Another sad point regarding these school closures has been specific to the fact that many of the schools that have closed are well known for their quality and their willingness to set up shop in urban center communities with limited schooling options. Most consequentially, however, they have been known as traditionally well serving poor black and Hispanic students and providing them with high-quality educational opportunities.

WHAT SCHOOL CHOICE LOOKS LIKE TODAY

Whereas it has been established that traditional iterations of school choice have been particularly focused upon fiscally autonomous public school districts and private schools, a contemporary era of education reform has ushered in new and expanded choices. Today, even larger numbers of families can avail themselves to school choice. Yet let's be very clear. A chasm is still present between those who have traditionally been able to take advantage of school choice alternatives and parents/caregivers residing in urban centers whose children continue to struggle in the absence of real and authentic school choice options.

In the modern-day United States, "the principal types of education privatization tried so far—charter schools, private scholarships, contracting out, tuition tax credits and deductions, homeschooling, and public vouchers"—have all been identified as rather promising school choice alternatives (Walberg and Bast, 2003, p. 235). Admittedly, however, some are more promising than others when it comes to aiding those children who are presently trapped in failing urban school districts.

Because of the fact that this book has, thus far, focused on providing urban center parents/caregivers an enhanced array of educational options, the remainder of this chapter will focus on four of the six forms of school choice broached in the preceding paragraph. They include charter schools, homeschooling, tuition tax credits and deductions, and school vouchers.

Charter Schools

Of all of the newly incorporated choices, charter schools might be considered the only such option that has truly made it into the mainstream. Following passage of the first charter school law in 1991, charter school legislation was passed in forty-three states and the District of Columbia by the fall of 2015 (IES/NCES, 2018a). The states in which public charter school legislation had not been enacted by that time included Kentucky, Montana, Nebraska, North Dakota, South Dakota, Vermont, and West Virginia (IES/NCES, 2018a).

On a national level, three US presidents (Bill Clinton, George W. Bush, and Barack Obama) all embraced charters as integral components of their education reform agendas. The philanthropic world followed suit with the Gates, Walton, and Broad Foundations helping to shine a national spotlight on charter schools, in addition to funding their innovative efforts to varying degrees (Bulkley, 2011).

So at this point, let's move gingerly to defining what makes a "charter school" a charter school.

> A *public charter school* is a publicly funded school that is typically governed by a group or organization under a legislative contract (or charter) with the state, district, or other entity. The charter exempts the school from certain state or local rules and regulations. In return for flexibility and autonomy, the charter school must meet the accountability standards outlined in its charter. A school's charter is reviewed periodically by the entity that granted it and can be revoked if guidelines on curriculum and management are not followed or if the accountability standards are not met. (IES/NCES, 2018a)

During AY 2000–2001 and AY 2015–2016, the percentage of US public charter schools spiked from 2 to 7 percent, with the total number of actual charter schools increasing from 2,000 to 6,900 (IES/NCES, 2018a). Additionally, the percentage of students attending public charter schools rose in a similar manner, going from 1 to 6 percent between the fall of 2000 and the fall of 2015 (IES/NCES, 2018a).

With respect to the student demographic composition of charter schools, the pupil population can be characterized in the following fashion. In 2014, 56.5 percent of charter schools were located in municipalities and 10 percent were located in rural regions (Caffee, 2018). During that year as well, California boasted of having the highest number of actual students enrolled in charters at 544,293. Washington, DC, had the largest percentage of attending students (42.7 percent), and Arizona had the second largest with 18 percent of its students attending charters (Caffee, 2018).

Last on the issue of charter school student demographics, 34.9 percent of white students attended in 2014. The next largest racial demographic was Hispanic students at 30 percent. Black students followed closely at the rate of 27.1 percent (Caffee, 2018). As has been fairly consistent with respect to school choice, Asian/Pacific Islander students maintained the lowest enrollment percentage at 4.1 percent. With respect to student eligibility for free and reduced lunch, 58.5 percent of charter school attendees were eligible (Caffee, 2018).

As previously indicated, there has been a great deal of attention given to the charter school movement. Yet that attention has also drawn a considerable number of opponents, in addition to a fairly steady stream of criticism. Some of the disparagements heard about charters include claims portraying charter schools as less transparent and accountable than traditional public schools, accusing them of cherry picking well-performing students from their local districts, and rejecting English Language Learning students and those with special needs because charters are ill equipped to meet their needs (National Alliance for Public Charter Schools, 2014).

It should be further noted that the vast majority of these allegations are refutable and there are copious statistics available that can be used to counter each of these contentions. In fairness, however, it must also be stated that charters aren't a panacea for all that ails public schooling. As with all other schools, there will necessarily be an unevenness in quality. But unlike other schools and resulting from a regular reauthorization process, it is highly likely that those charters that aren't up to par will not be reauthorized. Thus, there is a built-in quality control.

Another point regarding these flawed critiques is this. They have done little to dull the public's enthusiasm for charter schools. "The near universal finding is that parents of charter school students are much more satisfied with all respects of their children's schools than are comparable public school parents. The latter finding is, of course, exactly what economics predicts. Choice and competition work to a consumer's advantage and satisfaction" (Walberg and Bast, 2003, p. 239).

Homeschooling

Homeschooling is best illustrated as providing home instruction to children ranging in age from five to seventeen and with a grade equivalent between kindergarten and not higher than twelfth grade (IES/NCES, 2018b). The homeschooling choice serves as a viable alternative for a sizable group of US parents/caregivers and it is highly preferred by them, especially when juxtaposed against the option of sending their children to local public and/or private schools (IES/NCES, 2018b).

Back in the early 2000s, when this group of parents was surveyed and asked to identify the primary reasons undergirding their decisions to homeschool their children, they commonly expressed the belief that they could better educate their children at home. For the most part, it appears that they were right.

Interviews with actual homeschoolers from that time seem to confirm that their parents assigned weightier value to study skills, critical thinking, independent work, and love of learning than the students believed they would have received in a traditional brick-and-mortar school (Walberg and Bast, 2003). The students also reported that their homeschool teachers (their parents) put a greater emphasis on reading, writing, and mathematics than on extracurricular activities like gym, band, and study hall (Walberg and Bast, 2003).

While this all sounds wonderful in theory, homeschooling is difficult in practice. Not only does it require that parents be well educated themselves, it also requires that the family income be relatively high and stable. The homeschooling parent typically can't work a forty-hour workweek outside the home. Homeschooling the children is that parent's full-time job.

Further, homeschooling parents must be relatively well versed in state and local education requirements surrounding the homeschooling they provide to their children. Moreover, it is quite easy to err. For example, some homeschooling parents do their children a disservice by failing to learn their respective state's graduation requirements—that include physical education—and whether their children have fulfilled the state mandate.

More recent surveys of homeschooling parents—conducted during AY 2011–2012—revealed that a reported 91 percent of homeschooling parents cited concerns about the school environment as the single greatest factor influencing their decisions to homeschool. While homeschooling hasn't reached the level of popularity that public charter schools have, its approval is growing in some segments of the population.

During the span of years from 1983 to 2000, the homeschool population went from approximately 125,000 to a rough estimate of 1 million children (Walberg and Bast, 2003). As of 2016, about 3 percent of the school-age population was homeschooled during AY 2011–2012 (IES/NCES, 2018b).

The racial breakdown for this group is fairly predictable, with a higher percentage identifying as white (83 percent). Hispanic and black homeschoolers comprised 7 percent and 5 percent of the student demographic, respectively. Again, Asian or Pacific Islander students had the lowest homeschooling rate at 2 percent (IES/NCES, 2018b).

The most recent numbers on homeschooling include the following. Effective in the spring of 2016, there were approximately 2.3 million homeschooled students in the United States. This statistic represents growth as there were roughly 2 million home-educated children in the spring of 2010 (Ray, 2018). In consideration of these stats, it is safe to conjecture that the homeschool population is thriving and continues to grow. Data also support the finding that an approximate 3.4 million US adults were homeschooled at some point in their lives. Additionally, some adults within that group were homeschooled on average between six to eight years (Ray, 2018).

Last, although some might characterize "homeschooling" as one of education reform's most radical versions and suggest that "teaching one's children at home represents the most extreme form of decentralization and privatization in education" (Walberg and Bast, 2003, p. 245), it should be noted that it remains an infrequent choice for most urban center parents for many of the reasons previously broached in this section. So its growth is specific to the traditionally identified markets for school choice.

Tuition Tax Credits and Deductions

Tuition tax credits and deductions have proven to be among the least user-friendly options of school choice for low-SES parents/caregivers. Here's how they work. "Individual tax credits and deductions allow parents to receive state income tax relief for approved educational expenses, which can include private school tuition, books, supplies, computers, tutors and transportation" (EdChoice, 2018).

Whereas tax credits reduce the total amount of taxes an individual is obligated to pay, tax deductions slash that person's taxable income (EdChoice, 2018). With respect to tax credits, taxpayers would be compelled to apply in a preliminary fashion to a government agency for reimbursement on a K–12 expenditure that has already been made. Conversely, tax deductions would be filed at the point that the taxpayer files her/his personal income tax on April 15.

In the scheme of things, it is immaterial whether one is discussing tax credit or deduction plans as the bottom line is that both options necessitate parents/caregivers paying for their children's education and presenting proof of payment prior to the point that they can even be considered for reimbursement.

Further, the incentive is inconsistent and irregular. Tax credits and deductions aren't offered in all fifty states. In fact, some variation of these programs is available in only eight states. They are Alabama, Iowa, Illinois, Indiana, Louisiana, Minnesota, South Carolina, and Wisconsin (EdChoice, 2018). The average dollar amount of the tax credit might be as miniscule as Iowa's $116 or as generous as South Carolina's maximum allotment at $11,000. Another problem is particular to the fact that each state's eligibility requirements and plan details are different and idiosyncratic to that state's population and that population's needs.

So the most salient point to be ascertained from this discussion is that parents (even those considered cash strapped) would be required to pay their children's K–12 tuition up front and out of pocket before applying for or receiving either a tax credit or tax deduction. Thus, this approach to school choice becomes virtually useless to the low-income families that need it most.

"Requiring parents to pay out of pocket first and only afterward receive a tax credit or refund makes it more difficult for low- and middle-income parents to choose private schools. These are the very families that need the help most. Having to wait for a government refund check create[s] cash-flow problems for many poor households" (Walberg and Bast, 2003, p. 277).

Yet there's a very biased and elitist assumption that is implicit in the rationale for tax credits/tax deductions. We're assuming that the majority of low-income families are actually paying income taxes. There is a generally accepted notion that all parents/caregivers are working standard jobs and that relatively few of these families are receiving social service funding in order to keep their families afloat.

Thus, this option (in particular) possesses no inherent value for a substantial number of low-income families. As expressed earlier in this section, there is a contingency of parents/caregivers who simply can't afford to pay tuition first and receive the tax benefit many months later. "Even middle-income families benefit only to a small degree because their annual state income tax liabilities usually amount to a small fraction of the annual cost of a child's tuition at a private school" (Walberg and Bast, 2003, p. 243).

Yet we must also remember those parents who are paid under the table or receive welfare benefits and, as a result, do not pay income taxes. So what's the suggestion here? Is there a suggestion that tuition tax credits and deductions be eliminated from the existing array of school choice options? The answer here is a resounding "no!" After all, *Unlearning Failure* (in its entirety) has argued for expanded choice for all sectors of the parent/caregiver population as opposed to limiting such choices.

Therefore, there is a keen recognition that tax credits/deductions are wholly imperfect and perpetuate class-based discrimination against some sectors of parents/caregivers who have been historically victimized in this way. So the current plan must be revisited legislatively as well as logistically in order to make it more equitable and fairer. Another plausible fix would involve pairing it with the school choice alternative: vouchers (Walberg and Bast, 2003).

School Vouchers

The underpinnings of the concept that we currently reference as *school vouchers* or *educational savings plans* (as they're also known) can be found in the work of economist and philosopher Milton Friedman. Friedman, with his dispositions against big government and what he deemed unnecessary taxation, might be considered one of the first Libertarians to be identified as such. Some of his most influential writings were particular to the burden that government schooling imposed on all taxpayers, regardless of whether their children benefitted from it or not.

Friedman contended that subsidy provisions to families that could demonstrate need would be a more efficient way of financing public education. He stated that such subsidies would "eliminate the governmental machinery now required to collect tax funds from all residents during the whole of their lives and then pay it back mostly to the same people during the period when their children are in school" (Friedman, 1962, p. 87).

Friedman further purported that these subsidies would reinforce the temporary nature of such remedies, in addition to discouraging their long-term use (Friedman, 1962). They "would increase the likelihood that the subsidy component of school expenditures would decline as the need for such subsidies declined with increasing general levels of income" (Friedman, 1962, p. 87).

To his critics who suggested that vouchers or educational savings plans could never work in public education, he directed them to one of the first and most successful plans in US history, the GI Bill. Over time, school vouchers and education savings plans have gained in popularity. Currently, there are approximately thirty states with school voucher programs or similar approaches to private school choice in place.

In Gallup polls conducted during the 1980s, there was growing support for vouchers expressed by the general public. In 1992, Gallup determined that 71 percent of the general public, which included 88 percent of African Americans and 84 percent of Hispanics, supported school vouchers (Walberg and Bast, 2003). Today, slightly under half (43 percent) of the American public continues to support school vouchers for low-income students, according to the Hoover Institution (Prothero, 2017). This figure dropped from the rate of 55 percent four years ago (Prothero, 2017).

In the estimation of some, however, there was one surprising new finding in the most recent data released on the public appeal of vouchers. It now appears as if vouchers for low-income students stuck in failing schools are supported by more Democrats than Republicans. The Hoover Institution poll placed the percentages at 49 percent of Democrats to 37 percent of Republicans (Prothero, 2017).

Shockingly, these numbers have laid bare the disconnect between rank-and-file party members and the leaders of those political parties. For quite some time, Republican legislators have operated as the driving force behind voucher and other private school choice bills in state legislatures. Most times, their most ferocious pushback has been from Democrats (Prothero, 2017).

School vouchers have also been characterized as "the most radical form of privatization short of the free market" (Walberg and Bast, 2003, p. 246). Many school choice advocates consider them to be among the most promising options when it comes to leveling the playing field for urban center youngsters who have been historically relegated to the best education their ZIP codes could afford them as opposed to the highest quality education . . . period. It must also be acknowledged that voucher talk frequently ignites the most intense reaction from public school devotees and seemingly evokes the most fear in them as well.

The criticisms of detractors are predictable and consistent. Among the most popular critiques are that voucher programs siphon off money from the public schools that need the funding most (despite the fact that those schools have failed to improve regardless of the amounts of money thrown at them), as well as that they leave large numbers of special education students and English Language Learners behind without any recourse (Prothero, 2017). An interesting aside here is specific to the point that many of the same arguments used against vouchers have also been used to fight the proliferation of charter schools.

There is only one criticism that is distinctive to voucher programs exclusively, and it is that they violate the separation of church and state. If pressed, many voucher critics would admit that, although the argument is a powerful one, it is dated. Most importantly, however, the complaint has been litigated and it was legally decided that no such constitutional breach existed.

In *Zelman v. Simmons-Harris*, the US Supreme Court decreed in June 2002 that a state-enacted Cleveland, Ohio, school voucher program failed to infringe on the US Constitution's prohibition on government establishment of religion. It was determined that the voucher program served a valid secular purpose and was religion neutral.

Contrary to what public school advocates might believe, school voucher programs have a tradition of

> put[ting] parents in charge of choosing the best schools for their children. Parents receive tax-funded certificates or scholarships good for tuition (up to

some set amount) at participating schools, which must then compete for the parents' loyalty. . . . Of the various kinds of privatization discussed here, school vouchers represent the most potent type of reform. (Walberg and Bast, 2003, p. 246)

In conclusion, it remains germane that the need for school vouchers is most directly experienced in urban areas and, as *Unlearning Failure* has maintained throughout, these families simply have no more time to wait nor should they have to. They need relief now! If we (as a society) express the belief that inequitable schooling is the biggest civil rights issue of our time, then we have a collective responsibility to offer school choice and authentic educational options to all parents (regardless of where they live) without any additional delay.

References

Adams, D. W. (1998, February). Fundamental considerations: The deep meaning of Native American Schooling, 1880–1900. *Harvard Educational Review, 58*(1), 1–28.

Aiken, J. R., Salmon, E. D., and Hanges, P. J. (2013). The origins and legacy of the Civil Rights Act of 1964. *Journal of Business Psychology, 28*, 383–99.

Allington, R. L. (2013). What really matters when working with struggling readers. *The Reading Teacher, 66*(7), 520–30.

Altwerger, B. (2005). Reading for profit: A corporate coup in context. In B. Altwerger (Ed.), *Reading for profit: How the bottom line leaves kids behind* (pp. 1–10). Portsmouth, NH: Heinemann.

American Psychological Association. (2018). *Ethnic and racial minorities & socioeconomic status*. Washington, DC: American Psychological Association. Retrieved on August 24, 2018, from http://www.apa.org/pi/ses/resources/publications/

Anderson, J. D. (1988). *The education of Blacks in the South, 1860–1935*. Chapel Hill: The University of North Carolina Press.

Anyon, J. (1997). *Ghetto schooling: A political economy of urban educational reform*. New York: Teachers College Press.

Associated Press. (2018, May 25). Correction: Vatican-priest shortage story. *U.S. News & World Report*. Retrieved on August 27, 2018, from https://www.usnews.com/news/world/articles/2018-05-21/pope-laments-hemorrhaging-of-priests-and-nuns-in-europe

Banks, J. A. (1994). *Multiethnic education: Theory and practice* (third edition). Boston, MA: Allyn and Bacon.

Bell, D. (2005a). *Brown v. Board of Education* and the interest-convergence dilemma. In R. Delgado and J. Stefancic (Eds.), *The Derrick Bell reader* (pp. 33–39). New York: New York University Press.

Bell, D. (2005b). Serving two masters: Integration ideals and client interests in school desegregation litigation. In R. Delgado and J. Stefancic (Eds.), *The Derrick Bell reader* (pp. 99–109). New York: New York University Press.

Berg, N. (2012, March 26). U.S. urban population is up . . . but what does "urban" really mean? *Citylab*. Retrieved on August 24, 2018, from https://www.citylab.com/equity/2012/03/us-urban-population-what-does-urban-really-mean/1589/

Boaz, D. (1997). *Libertarianism: A primer*. New York: The Free Press.

Bowles, S., and Gintis, H. (1976). *Schooling in capitalist America: Educational reform and the contradictions of economic life*. New York: Basic.

Brown, F. (2004). The first serious implementation of *Brown*: The 1964 Civil Rights Act and beyond. *The Journal of Negro Education, 73*(3), 182–90.

References

Bulkley, K. E. (2011, Spring). Charter schools: Taking a closer look. *Kappa Delta Pi Record*, 110–15.

Bureau of the Census. (1993). *We the first Americans*. Washington, DC: Government Printing Office.

Bureau of Labor Statistics. (2018). *Economic news release: Union members summary*. Retrieved on June 20, 2018, from https://www.bls.gov/news.release/union2.nr0.htm

Caffee, A. (2018, May 10). Just the facts: Charter school statistics. *Niche*. Retrieved on August 28, 2018, from https://www.niche.com/blog/charter-school-statistics/

Camera, L. (2015a, October 28). Student scores in reading and math drop. *U.S. News & World Report*. Retrieved on May 29, 2018, from https://www.usnews.com/news/articles/2015/10/28/student-scores-in-reading-and-math-drop

Camera, L. (2015b, October 29). Students in urban school districts lagging in math, reading. *U.S. News & World Report*. Retrieved on May 29, 2018, from https://www.usnews.com/news/blogs/data-mine/2015/10/29/urban-school-districts-post-lackluster-math-and-reading-scores

Carruthers, J. H. (1994). Black intellectuals and the crisis in black education. In M. J. Shujaa (Ed.), *Too much schooling, too little education: A paradox of black life in white societies* (pp. 37–55). Trenton, NJ: Africa World Press.

Chubb, J. E., and Moe, T. M. (1990). *Politics, markets, and America's schools*. Washington, DC: Brookings Institution.

Clark, A. (2017, May 8). Top democrat wants $125M more for N.J. schools in new plan. *NJ.com*. http://www.nj.com/education/2017/05/nj_school_funding_battle_democrats_christie_fair_f.html

Collins, R. (1977). Some comparative principles of educational stratification. *Harvard Educational Review, 47*(1), 1–27.

Council for American Private Education. (2018). *FAQs about private schools*. Retrieved on August 25, 2018, from http://www.capenet.org/facts.html

DoSomething.org. (2018). *11 facts about high school dropout rates*. Retrieved on August 1, 2018, from https://www.dosomething.org/us/facts/11-facts-about-high-school-dropout-rates

Donato, R. (1997). The other struggle for equal schools: Mexican Americans during the Civil Rights era. Albany: SUNY Press.

DuBois, W. E. B. (1990). *The souls of black folk*. New York: Vintage Books/Library of America.

EdChoice. (2018). Types of school choice: How do K–12 education tax credits and deductions work? https://www.edchoice.org/school-choice/types-of-school-choice/how-do-k-12-education-tax-credits-deductions-work/

Edelsky, C., and Bomer, R. (2005). Heads they win; Tails we lose. In B. Altwerger (Ed.), *Reading for profit: How the bottom line leaves kids behind* (pp. 11–20). Portsmouth, NH: Heinemann.

Elementaryschools.org. (2018). *Elementaryschools.org: Shepaug Valley Middle School*. https://elementaryschools.org/directory/ct/cities/washington/shepaug-valley-middle-school/90353000733/.

Field, A. J. (1976). Educational expansion in mid-nineteenth-century Massachusetts: Human capital formation or structural reinforcement? *Harvard Educational Review, 46*(4), 521–52.

Finn, J. D., and Servoss, T. J. (2015). Security measures and discipline in American high schools. In D. J. Losen (Ed.), *Closing the school discipline gap: Equitable remedies for excessive exclusion* (pp. 44–58). New York: Teachers College Press.

Fortin, J. (2018, July 4). "Access to literacy" is not a constitutional right, judge in Detroit rules. Retrieved on July 14, 2018, from https://www.nytimes.com/2018/07/04/education/detroit-public-schools-education.html?hpw&rref=education&action=click&pgtype=Homepage&module=well-region&region=bottom-well&WT.nav=bottom-well

Friedman, M. (1962, 1982, 2002). *Capitalism and freedom* (fortieth anniversary edition). Chicago: The University of Chicago Press.

Gamson, D. (2007). From progressivism to federalism: The pursuit of equal educational opportunity, 1915–1965. In C. F. Kaestle and A. E. Lodewick (Eds.), *To educate a nation: Federal and national strategies of school reform* (pp. 177–201). New York: The Free Press.

Garan, E. (2005). Scientific flimflam: A who's who of entrepreneurial research. In B. Altwerger (Ed.), *Reading for profit: How the bottom line leaves kids behind* (pp. 21–32). Portsmouth, NH: Heinemann.

Gee, J. P., and Hayes, E. R. (2011). *Language and learning in the digital age.* London: Routledge.

Geppert, J. (2017, May 18). Three very different flavors for NJ school funding. *Observer.com.* http://observer.com/2017/05/three-very-different-flavors-for-nj-school-funding/

Gibson, D. (2017, December 6). U.S. nuns on the decline as fewer and fewer women take up religious orders. *HuffPost.* Retrieved on August 27, 2018, from https://www.huffingtonpost.com/2014/10/14/us-nuns-decline_n_5982888.html

Gladwell, M. (2013). *David and Goliath: Underdogs, misfits, and the art of battling giants.* New York: Back Bay Books, Little Brown and Company.

Grossberg, B. (2017, February 13). Profile for "A Better Chance": Making private school accessible for all students. *ThoughtCo.* https://www.thoughtco.com/students-of-color-best-private-schools-2774294

Havard, C. J. (2009). Funny money: How federal education funding hurts poor and minority students. In *ScholarWorks@University of Baltimore School of Law*, 123–47.

Hauser, C. (2017, December 6). Too many children in California can't read, lawsuit claims. *New York Times.* Retrieved on July 14, 2018, from https://www.nytimes.com/2017/12/06/us/california-literacy-lawsuit.html?action=click&module=RelatedCoverage&pgtype=Article&region=Footer

Heilbroner, R. (1989, January 23). The triumph of capitalism. *The New Yorker.* Retrieved on July 30, 2018, from https://www.newyorker.com/magazine/1989/01/23/the-triumph-of-capitalism

Hershberg, T., and Robertson-Kraft, C. (Eds.) (2009). *A grand bargain for education reform: New rewards and supports for new accountability.* Cambridge, MA: Harvard Education Press.

Hoxby, C. M. (1998, March). What do America's "traditional" forms of school choice teach us about school choice reforms? *FRBNY Economic Policy Review*, 47–59.

IES/National Center for Education Statistics. (2018a). *Fast Facts: Charter Schools.* https://nces.ed.gov/fastfacts/display.asp?id=30

IES/National Center for Education Statistics. (2018b). *Fast Facts: Homeschooling.* https://nces.ed.gov/fastfacts/display.asp?id=91

IES/National Center for Education Statistics. (2018c). *Private school enrollment.* https://nces.ed.gov/programs/coe/indicator_cgc.asp

Illich, I. (1971). *Deschooling society.* London and New York: Marion Boyers.

Jeffrey, T. P. (2012, September 10). U.S. department of education: 79% of Chicago 8th graders not proficient in reading. *CNSNEWS.com.* Retrieved on May 29, 2018, from https://www.cnsnews.com/news/article/us-department-education-79-chicago-8th-graders-not-proficient-reading

Jepsen, C. (2015). Class size: Does it matter for student achievement? *IZA World of Labor 2015, 190*, 1–10.

Kaestle, C. F. (2007). Federal education policy and the changing national polity for education, 1957–2007. In C. F. Kaestle and A. E. Lodewick (eds.), *To educate a nation: Federal and national strategies of school reform* (17–40). Lawrence: University Press of Kansas.

Katz, M. (1971, 1975). *Class, bureaucracy, and schools: The illusion of educational change in America.* New York: Praeger.

Kelley, R. D. G. (1997). *Yo' mama's disfunktional!* Boston: The Beacon Press.

Kerr, J. C. (2015, October 28). Math, reading scores slip for nation's school kids. *NBCChicago.com.* Retrieved on May 29, 2018, from https://www.nbcchicago.com/news/national-international/Math-Reading-Scores-Slip-for-Nations-School-Kids--337954092.html

Klarman, M. J. (1994, June). How *Brown* changed race relations: The backlash thesis. *Journal of American History*, 81–118.

Krueger, N. F., and Brazeal, D. V. (1994). Entrepreneurial potential and potential entrepreneurs. *Entrepreneurship theory and practice, 18*, 91–104.

References

Ladson-Billings, G. (2004). Landing on the wrong note: The price we paid for *Brown*. *Educational Researcher, 33*(7), 3–13.

Lake, R. (2016, May 12). *Shocking facts: 23 statistics on illiteracy in America*. http://www.creditdonkey.com/illiteracy-in-america.html

Legal Information Institute. (2018, February 7). Federalism. https://www.law.cornell.edu/wex/federalism

Lewis, L. (2016, June 3). Title I is supposed to fund our poorest schools. *Slate*. Retrieved on April 20, 2018, from http://www.slate.com/articles/life/education/2016/06/title_i_funding_often_still_doesn_t_make_it_to_our_poorest_schools_half.html

Lewis, S. D. (2015a, October 28). Detroit worst in math, reading scores among big cities. *Detroit News*. Retrieved on May 28, 2018, from https://www.detroitnews.com/story/news/local/detroit-city/2015/10/28/national-assessment-educational-progress-detroit-math-reading-results/74718372/.

Lewis, S. D. (2015b, October 28). Michigan test score gains worst in nation. *Detroit News*. Retrieved on May 28, 2018, from https://www.detroitnews.com/story/news/local/michigan/2017/02/20/michigan-test-score-gains-worst-nation/98144368/

Malinconico, J. (2017, May 16). About 85 Paterson teachers get layoff notices. *Northjersey.com*. http://www.northjersey.com/story/news/paterson-press/2017/05/16/85-paterson-teachers-get-layoff-notices-union-says/324745001/

Manna, P., and Ryan, L. L. (2011). Competitive grants and educational federalism: President Obama's Race to the Top program in theory and practice. *Publius: The Journal of Federalism, 41*(3), 522–46

Martin, R., and McClure, P. (1969). *Title I of ESEA: Is it helping poor children?* Washington, DC: Washington Research Project and NAACP Legal Defense and Educational Fund, Inc.

Meyer, J. W., Tyack, D., Nagel, J., and Gordon, A. (1979). Public education as nation-building in America: Enrollments and bureaucratization in the American states, 1870–1930. *American Journal of Sociology, 85*(3), 591–613.

Mill, J. S. (1848). Objections to government interference. In D. Boaz (Ed.), *The Libertarian reader: Classic & contemporary writings from Lao-Tzu to Milton Friedman* (pp. 25–27). New York: The Free Press.

Morrison, T. (1992). *Playing in the dark: Whiteness and the literary imagination*. New York: Vintage Books.

Moshinsky, B. (2017, January 12). The 19 countries that hold the most U.S. debt. *Business Insider*. http://www.businessinsider.com/us-treasury-countries-hold-the-most-us-debt-2017-1

National Alliance for Public Charter Schools. (2014). *Separating fact & fiction: What you need to know about charter schools*. Washington, DC: National Alliance for Public Charter Schools.

National Assessment of Educational Progress. (2017a). *About the Trial Urban District Assessment (TUDA)*. Retrieved on June 4, 2018, from https://nces.ed.gov/nationsreportcard/about/district.aspx.

National Assessment of Educational Progress. (2017b). *The nation's report card newsroom*. Retrieved on June 4, 2018, from https://www.nationsreportcard.gov/media.aspx

National Constitution Center (2018, June 4). *Supreme Court scorecard: The spring 2018 edition (updated 6/4/2018)*. Retrieved on June 10, 2018, from https://www.yahoo.com/news/supreme-court-scorecard-spring-2018-edition-updated-6-130300217--politics.html.

New Jersey League of Municipalities. (2017, May 22). *Local property taxes and New Jersey state government 2013*. http://www.njslom.org/SG-Property_Taxes.html

NorthJersey.com. (2017, February 28). Full text of Christie's final budget address. *NorthJersey.com*. http://www.northjersey.com/story/news/new-jersey/2017/02/28/full-text-christies-final-budget-address/98534734/

Noguera, P. (2003). *City schools and the American dream: Reclaiming the promise of public education*. New York: Teachers College Press.

Ogbu, J. U. (2003). *Black American students in an affluent suburb: A study of academic disengagement*. Mahwah, NJ: Lawrence Erlbaum Associates, Publishers.

Onosko, J. (2011). Race to the Top leaves children and future citizens behind: The devastating effects of centralization, standardization, and high stakes accountability. *Democracy & Education, 19*(2), 1–11. https://democracyeducationjournal.org/home/vol19/iss2/

Orfield, G., Ee, J., and Coughlan, R. (2017, November). *New Jersey's segregated schools: Trends and paths forward.* UCLA: The Civil Rights Project/Proyecto Derechos Civiles.

Paul, D. G. (2000). *Raising black children who love reading and writing: A guide from birth through grade 6.* Westport, CT: Bergin and Garvey/Greenwood Publishing Group.

Paul, D. G. (2001). *Life, culture and education on the academic plantation: Womanist thought and perspective.* New York: Peter Lang.

Paul, D. (2016, Fall). Millennial morphing of the digital divide and its implications for African American youngsters in a new literacies era (Commentary). *Journal of Negro Education, 85*(4), 407–11.

Paul, D. G. (2017). *Beyond tolerance: Real world literacy teaching and learning, PreK–6.* Lanham, MD: Rowman & Littlefield.

Popkewitz, T. S. (1997). The production of reason and power: Curriculum history and intellectual traditions. *Journal of Curriculum Studies, 29*(2), 131–64.

ProLiteracy America (2003). *U.S. adult literacy programs: Making a difference: A review of research on positive outcomes achieved by literacy programs and the people they serve.* Syracuse, NY: US Programs Division of ProLiteracy Worldwide.

Prothero, A. (2017, January 26). What are school vouchers and how do they work? *Education Week.* Retrieved on August 30, 2018, from https://www.edweek.org/ew/issues/vouchers/index.html

Rahman, J. (2015, March 26). School district will not raise local taxes, but will cut 363 jobs. *Patersontimes.com.* http://patersontimes.com/2015/03/26/school-district-will-not-raise-local-taxes-but-will-cut-363-jobs/

Ray, B. D. (2018, January 13). *Research facts on homeschooling: Homeschool fast facts.* Salem, OR: National Home Education Research Institute. Retrieved on August 28, 2018, from https://www.nheri.org/research-facts-on-homeschooling/

Riley, J. L. (2014). *Please stop helping us: How liberals make it harder for blacks to succeed.* New York: Encounter Books.

Rist, R. C. (1973). *The urban school: A factory for failure.* Cambridge, MA: MIT Press.

Rinde, M. (2016, April 13). Reformers question if school-aid formula is out of touch with reality. *NJSpotlight.com.* http://www.njspotlight.com/stories/16/04/12/reformers-question-if-school-aid-formula-is-out-of-touch-with-reality/.

Robelen, E. W. (2005, April 13). 40 years after ESEA, federal role in schools is broader than ever. *Education Week.* http://www.edweek.org/ew/articles/2005/04/13/31esea.h24.html

Rotherham, A. (1999). Toward performance-based federal education funding: Reauthorization of the Elementary and Secondary Education Act. *Progressive Policy Institute,* 1–23.

Saad, L. (2018, April 9). Catholics' Church attendance resumes downward slide. *Gallup.* Retrieved on August 25, 2018, from https://news.gallup.com/poll/232226/church-attendance-among-catholics-resumes-downward-slide.aspx.

Sabatini, J. (2015, December). *Understanding the basic reading skills of U.S. adults: Reading components in the PIAAC Literacy Survey.* Princeton, NJ: Educational Testing Service.

Schanzenbach, D. W. (2014). *Does class size matter?* Boulder, CO: National Education Policy Center. Retrieved March 6, 2018, from http://nepc.colorado.edu/publication/does-class-size-matter

Shollenberger, T. L. (2015). Racial disparities in school suspensions and subsequent outcomes: Evidence from the National Longitudinal Survey of Youth. In D. J. Losen, (Ed.), *Closing the school discipline gap: Equitable remedies for excessive exclusion* (pp. 31–43). New York: Teachers College Press.

Simon, R., and Overberg, P. (2016, September 1). Blacks lag in business ownership, but gap is narrowing. *Wall Street Journal.* https://www.wsj.com/articles/blacks-lag-in-business-ownership-but-gap-is-narrowing-1472702465

Soergel, A. (2016, December 8). In America's rural-urban divide, age, earnings and education are prominent. *U.S. News & World Report.* Retrieved on August 25, 2018, from https://

www.usnews.com/news/articles/2016-12-08/in-americas-rural-urban-divide-age-earnings-and-education-are-prominent

Stanmyre, M., and Politi, S. (2017a, February 24). New questions, including human trafficking concerns, broadside N.J. basketball power. *NJ.com*. http://www.nj.com/sports/index.ssf/2017/02/new_questions_including_human_trafficking_concerns.html.

Stanmyre, M., and Politi, S. (2017b, March 8). School forged transcripts in Paterson hoops scandal. See the documents. *NJ.com*. http://www.nj.com/sports/index.ssf/2017/03/forged_transcript_raises_more_paterson_eastside_co.html

StateAidGuy (2015, July 31). The problems of PILOTs. *New Jersey education aid: Exposing the savage inequalities of New Jersey's education aid distribution*. http://njeducationaid.blogspot.com/2015/07/the-problems-of-pilots.html

Sweeney, S. (2017, June 23). Sweeney: School aid must be based on actual enrollment. *APP.com*. http://www.app.com/story/opinion/columnists/2017/06/23/steve-sweeney-school-aid-enrollment/103141370/.

Tatum, B. D. (1997). *Why are all of the Black kids sitting together in the cafeteria? And other conversations about race*. New York: Perseus Books Group.

Teale, W. H., Paciga, K. A., and Hoffman, J. L. (2007). Beginning reading instruction in urban schools: The curriculum gap ensures a continuing achievement gap. *The Reading Teacher*, *61*(4), 344–48.

Thomas, J. Y., and Brady, K. P. (2016, September 18). Chapter 3: The Elementary and Secondary Education Act at 40: Equity, accountability, and the evolving federal role in public education. *Review of Research in Education, 29*, 51–67. http://rre.aera.net

Toldson, I. A., McGee, T., and Lemmons, B. P. (2015). Reducing suspensions by improving academic engagement among school-age black males. In D. J. Losen (Ed.), *Closing the school discipline gap: Equitable remedies for excessive exclusion* (pp. 107–17). New York: Teachers College Press.

Tyack, D., and Cuban, L. (1995). *Tinkering toward utopia: A century of public school reform*. Cambridge, MA: Harvard University Press.

Universal Income Project. (2016). About. *Universal Income Project*. Retrieved on July 30, 2018, from https://www.universalincome.org/about/

US Department of Education. (2002). *Reading first guidance*. Washington, DC: US Department of Education.

US General Accounting Office. (2002, January). *GAO-02-242: Title I funding: Poor children benefit through funding per poor child differs*. Washington, DC: US General Accounting Office.

Walberg, H. J., and Bast, J. L. (2003). *Education and capitalism: How overcoming our fear of markets and economics can improve America's schools*. Stanford, CA: Hoover Institution Press.

Walstad, W. B., and Kourilsky, M. L. (1998). Entrepreneurial attitudes and knowledge of black youth. *Entrepreneurship Theory and Practice, 23*, 5–18.

Webb, L. D. (2006). *The history of American education: A great American experiment*. Upper Saddle River, NJ: Pearson Merrill Prentice Hall.

Witte, J. F. (2000). *The market approach to education*. Princeton, NJ: Princeton University Press.

About the Author

Dierdre G. Paul, EdD and full professor, recently marked her twenty-fifth year of teaching at Montclair State University with no signs of slowing down. Dierdre is the author of five books, four book chapters, and multiple journal articles, in addition to giving regular testimony before the New Jersey State Legislature and making presentations before groups of teachers, parents, and academics. Her most significant contribution, however, is raising two successful adults as a single, divorced mom.

www.ingramcontent.com/pod-product-compliance
Lightning Source LLC
Chambersburg PA
CBHW030146240426
43672CB00005B/285